T0021915

Praise for *Loneliness*

We have been in vocational ministry for over forty years and have never seen a rise in loneliness like today. The ache in people's souls has jumped dramatically since the pandemic. And no one seems to be talking about an answer to this ache until now. In this book, Steve will take you on a journey through his battle with loneliness that you will relate to, but you will also find a God who meets us right in the middle of this loneliness. We've never heard a pastor speak or write so honestly about this struggle, but Steve goes there. And we mean, really goes there. And he will take you there as well. And you will find healing just as he did. Buckle up because God is about to meet you right where you are. It's a journey we all need to take.

DAVE & ANN WILSON, cohosts of *FamilyLife Today*

This book is badly needed. Due to changes in the way we work and worship, we are more isolated than ever. Indeed, loneliness has become a pandemic. But Steve DeWitt knows that the loneliness we all feel is also an opportunity for us to experience God's grace in life-giving ways. In this wise, practical, and hope-filled book, he shows us how to see our loneliness in gospel perspective and respond in ways that bring health and healing.

PHILIP RYKEN, President, Wheaton College

A fascinating look at loneliness from a biblical perspective. With increasing urbanization and social fragmentation in our premodern Global South societies, loneliness is fast becoming a growing concern. Steve Dewitt has given us a warm, inspirational and gentle guide that reads like a conversation with a trusted friend.

OSCAR MURIU, pastor of Nairobi Chapel, Nairobi, Kenya

You might be married with kids and boast thousands of friends on social media. Yet you might still feel lonely. Steve DeWitt challenged me by showing how loneliness can be a gift from God to help us love Him more fully. Readers will join me in learning to take loneliness as an occasion to turn toward our ever-present God.

COLLIN HANSEN, editor-in-chief of The Gospel Coalition and host of the *Gospelbound* podcast

As a settled widow of twenty years, I can highly recommend this book to anyone suffering loneliness due to loss of a loved one or in any situation of loneliness. It is practical and engaging, chock-full of biblical truth that leads us to the principle of redeeming loneliness and seeing it as a gift from God that points us to Him. If you need hope, you will find it here.

DONNA CUNNINGHAM, widow and member of Bethel Church, NW Indiana

Working with young adults on a college campus, loneliness is a pervasive feeling expressed daily, and the world is providing empty solutions. With a beautiful blend of biblical wisdom and practical insight, Steve DeWitt unpacks the origins of loneliness in each of us and offers transformative solutions rooted in the gospel of Jesus Christ. Through heartfelt personal stories and scriptural truths, readers are guided toward a deeper understanding of loneliness and our intrinsic need for a relationship with God and others. This book provides a path to contentment amidst life's challenges.

DREW FLAMM, President, Grace College & Seminary

The first time I met Steve, the first thing I said to him during our lunch was, "Tell me about your family." Of course, I was unaware that Steve was single at the time . . . So I've known Steve from his days as the "single megachurch pastor" and now as the "married with children megachurch pastor." Through it all, I've witnessed Steve use his singleness, his marriage, and his parenting all for the glory of God. My friend, my pastor, my ministry colleague—Steve DeWitt—has that same "it's all about Him" focus in his biblical, realistic book, *Loneliness*. Single or married, younger or older, this book is for all of us because it gets to the heart of loneliness and walks us through all the various stages and phases of loneliness. But *Loneliness* doesn't leave you alone. It gently leads you to your gentle Shepherd who will never leave you or forsake you. In His presence, we can lament our loneliness without hating it, and use our loneliness without wasting it.

BOB KELLEMEN, author of *Gospel-Centered Marriage Counseling* and *Gospel-Centered Family Counseling*

In this thoughtful book, Steve DeWitt shares his own transformative journey with loneliness. With warmth, biblical insight, and a focus on practical action, *Loneliness* helps readers see their challenging solitary times as catalysts for growth and deeper connections with others. This is a truly valuable resource that speaks to the redemptive power of God available in our darkest moments.

SHAWN THORNTON, Senior Pastor, Calvary Community Church, Westlake Village, CA

Loneliness

Don't Hate It
or Waste It
Redeem It

Steve DeWitt

MOODY PUBLISHERS
CHICAGO

© 2024 by
STEVE DEWITT

All rights reserved. No part of this book may be reproduced in any form without permission in writing from the publisher, except in the case of brief quotations embodied in critical articles or reviews.

Unless otherwise indicated, all Scripture quotations are from the ESV® Bible (The Holy Bible, English Standard Version®), © 2001 by Crossway, a publishing ministry of Good News Publishers. Used by permission. All rights reserved. The ESV text may not be quoted in any publication made available to the public by a Creative Commons license. The ESV may not be translated in whole or in part into any other language.

Scripture quotations marked (NIV) are taken from the Holy Bible, New International Version®, NIV®. Copyright © 1973, 1978, 1984, 2011 by Biblica, Inc.™ Used by permission of Zondervan. All rights reserved worldwide. www.zondervan.com The "NIV" and "New International Version" are trademarks registered in the United States Patent and Trademark Office by Biblica, Inc.™

Scripture quotations marked KJV are taken from the King James Version.

Some content has been adapted from the author's articles on Desiring God and The Gospel Coalition and a sermon series from Bethel Church.

Edited by Connor Sterchi
Interior design: Brandi Davis
Cover design: Tammy Adelhardt
Cover design of city landscape copyright © 2023 by Marina Zlochin/Adobe Stock (268964943). All rights reserved.

Library of Congress Cataloging-in-Publication Data

Names: DeWitt, Steve (Senior Pastor), author.
Title: Loneliness : don't hate it or waste it, redeem it / by Steve DeWitt.

Description: Chicago : Moody Publishers, [2024] | Includes bibliographical
    references. | Summary: "In a time when loneliness is at an all-time
    high, Loneliness-rich with biblical truth and practical help-speaks to
    all hearts. Writing on topics that affect us and the ones we love,
    DeWitt shows us the way out of our pain and into relational flourishing
    with God and others"-- Provided by publisher.
Identifiers: LCCN 2023053272 (print) | LCCN 2023053273 (ebook) | ISBN
    9780802432186 | ISBN 9780802472830 (ebook)
Subjects: LCSH: Loneliness--Biblical teaching. | Loneliness--Religious
    aspects--Christianity. | Spiritual life--Christianity. | BISAC: RELIGION
    / Christian Living / Inspirational | RELIGION / Christian Living /
    Death, Grief, Bereavement
Classification: LCC BV4911 .D495 2024 (print) | LCC BV4911 (ebook) | DDC
    248.8/6--dc23/eng/20240207
LC record available at https://lccn.loc.gov/2023053272
LC ebook record available at https://lccn.loc.gov/2023053273

Originally delivered by fleets of horse-drawn wagons, the affordable paperbacks from D. L. Moody's publishing house resourced the church and served everyday people. Now, after more than 125 years of publishing and ministry, Moody Publishers' mission remains the same—even if our delivery systems have changed a bit. For more information on other books (and resources) created from a biblical perspective, go to www.moodypublishers.com or write to:

Moody Publishers
820 N. LaSalle Boulevard
Chicago, IL 60610

1 3 5 7 9 10 8 6 4 2

Printed in the United States of America

Dedication

It is my delight to dedicate this book
to my dear friends

Larry and Patti Green
Kurt and Kelly Hand
Bob and Wendy Smith &
Doug and Marcia VandeGutche

for your loving friendship
over the years and to

Jennifer, Kiralee, and Madeline

for helping me redeem my loneliness every day.

For I have derived much joy and comfort from your love . . .
(Philemon 1:7)

Contents

Introduction

I WAS DRIVING DOWN the interstate somewhere near Des Moines, Iowa. I was in my early twenties and in graduate school at the time. My life thus far was humming along nicely. My Christian upbringing grounded my life in the gospel and the Christian worldview. I was a spiritually minded young man earnest about following Christ. I had made my way through college successfully as an honors student and president of the student body, including friendships with both men and women that I treasured.

Yet I was surprised to exit college single. My parents had married during college, and I showed up while Dad was working on his master's degree. I assumed a similar path in my life. I dated a lot, but for some reason, no relationship rose to the "let's get married" level.

Let me clarify something early here: this is not a marriage-takes-care-of-loneliness book. My years of singleness were the context for carefully assessing my aloneness and loneliness. Your journey in loneliness may be different and likely is. I'll share my story with you throughout this book and hope for significant points of commonality with yours.

I wasn't too concerned. Life lay ahead of me, filled with opportunities, potential relationships, and, hopefully, a family. As I drove along that interstate, a song came on the radio. I had never heard it before, but it struck a chord with me as it bypassed my defense shields and went straight to the core fears of my heart. The title of the song was "Alone Again, Naturally."

The lyrics tell the story of the songwriter's dismay at his life. Each stanza repeats the song title, "Alone again, naturally." One particular lyric stands out: "If He really does exist, why did He desert me in my hour of need?" His conclusion? I am "alone again, naturally."

As I listened, the thought struck me and stuck with me all these years later: What if my future is to be alone? The song, and the idea, proved prophetic.

THE LONELY SINGLE MEGACHURCH PASTOR

Little did I know when I heard that song, stretching before me were 8,000 nights alone. I was far from alone in my public life as a pastor. In God's providence, I would serve as senior pastor of Bethel Church in northwest Indiana through my thirties and early forties and see the church become what is commonly called a megachurch (while I don't love this term, I use it simply to explain my story). Megachurch experts Scott Thumma and Warren Bird claimed I was likely the only never-married megachurch pastor in America.[1] Yes, I was surrounded by people all the time. My role provided opportunities for ministry outside our local church, and my life had a sheen of success and relationships that, from the outside, seemed fulfilled. It was, to an extent.

My private life was a very different relational experience. Privately I continued to hope for a spouse and family that I assumed would fill that gnawing ache in my heart. I tried. My public role brought me proximity to godly single Christian women. In retrospect, my singleness was too often my own doing and most often caused by my fears, which constantly torpedoed what otherwise would likely have been a healthy family experience.

This put me in a unique place, socially connected with thousands of people yet feeling very much alone.

I spent those 8,000 nights of adulthood alone (a roommate here or there, notwithstanding), filtering my experience through my grid of pastor-theologian. Somewhere along the way, I began thinking more deeply, and I trust biblically, about the powerful ache my aloneness perpetuated within me. What is this nagging emotion I feel? Why does it hurt so much? What fuels it? Is there a cause or cure? How should my Christian faith and the gospel of Jesus intersect with my loneliness?

THE LONELY MARRIED MEGACHURCH PASTOR

Lest you read this as a "single people are lonely" book, let me tell you the rest of the story. I owe loneliness a great debt as it did bring me a wife and children in a most unusual way. One day I experienced a painful reminder of a past broken relationship. I was seized with regret and sorrow, which created a tsunami wave of loneliness and despair. Upon arriving home, I sat at my computer and wrote my thoughts and feelings about loneliness. I submitted the article to The Gospel Coalition website editors. They published it under the title "Lonely Me: A Pastoral Perspective on Loneliness." The article had a remarkable readership around the world. I heard from lonely people worldwide, many of them single women wondering if they might help me with my loneliness.

The article made its way to Kansas City, Missouri, where friends of mine shared it with a single woman, a friend of theirs. This woman, Jennifer, had recently shared with their church her struggles with singleness and fulfillment. My friend shared my article along with an inquiry if she would like to meet me. This led to an introduction and a fast and furious romance. I asked Jennifer to marry me from our church's auditorium stage at the end of a worship service. She graciously said yes, and three months later, we were married. Wonderfully, God provided two daughters within three years, and we have passed the eleven-year marriage mark. Given what came to me providentially from that article, I owe my loneliness a significant thank-you. If you take to heart the biblical principles in this book, I hope that someday you, too, can be thankful for your loneliness. I hope to set you on a journey from loneliness as an enemy to loneliness as a guide and friend. You don't need to hate it, as painful as it is. God wants loneliness to have its powerful redemptive effect in our lives.

UNLESS WE UNDERSTAND BIBLICALLY WHAT LONELINESS IS AND WHY WE ARE LONELY, WE WILL UNCONSCIOUSLY INFLAME IT AND ALLOW IT TO RULE AND RUIN OUR LIVES.

I share this to make something abundantly clear: even with a loving wife, wonderful daughters, and an excellent and expansive church family, I, Steve DeWitt, am still lonely. I am lonely in different ways and to different degrees. Yet, what is clear experientially and biblically is that marriage and children are not the cure for loneliness. Some of the loneliest people are married people. Aloneness and loneliness are found in all categories and seasons of life—single, married, youth, seasoned, widowed, divorced, around family or not. Loneliness is existentially slippery. Unless we under-stand biblically what loneliness is and why we are lonely, we will unconsciously inflame it and allow it to rule and ruin our lives.

Through Jesus, God offers a better way.

Throughout this book, I will urge you to do something with your loneliness. You may think you will always feel this pain. No. You don't have to. Loneliness is a gift from God. Don't hate it. Don't waste it. Use it. Redeem it. How? Read on.

The Genesis
of Loneliness

AN ADAGE GOES, what can you know if you see a turtle on top of a post? Someone put it there. If an entire ranch had a turtle on every post, you could safely deduce that the rancher had a purpose. One could be a fluke. All of them indicate a purpose.

The reality of human loneliness is so pervasive and powerful, like the turtle, there must be a reason. A government agency produced a careful survey of who Americans are spending their time with. It turns out, mostly no one.

The 2020 pandemic exacerbated an already existing national health crisis. As I wrote this book, study after study was published saying the same reality: we are a crazy lonely society. One indicator shows that more Americans are living alone than ever.[1] Even our dining together isn't what it used to be, with Americans eating 40 percent of their meals alone.[2] A sociologist summarized the findings: "It's just a stunning social change. . . . I came to see it as the biggest demographic change in the last century that we failed to recognize and take seriously."[3]

Further, loneliness significantly diminishes us both emotionally and physically. Recent studies indicate a correlation between the number of social interactions and the health of our brains.[4] People with fewer social connections had smaller brains; correlatively, those with more had larger brains. Researchers at the University of Pennsylvania write, "Social isolation has been associated with . . . premature mortality, increased risk of coronary heart disease and stroke, increased reporting of depressive symptoms, as well as increased dementia risk."[4] Recent terms like "doomscrolling" (frenetic social media surfing of bad news) and "bed rotting" (a coping mechanism of isolation and obsessive media consumption) were neither heard of nor practiced in all of human history. While pathologies have always been with us, technology provides faux intimacies and perceived soul care as never before. Contemporary sociologists' alarm bells ring consistent with the ancient story of humanity from the biblical text.

Actor Matthew Perry's tragic death in his hot tub brought news reports of his profound loneliness. Perry made his fame and fortune acting on the show *Friends*. It was a massive comedy hit, not only for its humor but also for the camaraderie and community it depicted. In some ways it is a metaphor for friendships in the twenty-first century in which we often portray ourselves as having robust relationships and friend circles online, appearing to be fulfilled, while privately enduring relational emptiness.

Scripture tells the story of loneliness. Loneliness is one of the many consequences of the fall, when sin invaded humanity and has left brokenness and destruction in its wake ever since. Not that loneliness is a sin! One of my goals with this book is to help you see loneliness as a consequence of humanity's fall into sin but not sin itself. It is a gracious gift from God that can draw us back to Him and others. Relational pain and strain weren't always a part of our story. The book of Genesis begins the story of loneliness with the account of God's creation of humanity.

> Then God said, "Let us make man in our image, after our likeness. And let them have dominion over the fish of the sea and over the birds of the heavens and over the livestock and over all the earth and over every creeping thing that creeps on the earth." So God created man in his own image, in the image of God he created him; male and female he created them. (Gen. 1:24–27)

Adam is God's final act of creation, indeed, His masterpiece. We know this because far greater detail is given about the how and why of Adam's creation than anything else God created. Note how the narrative slows down by providing the intra-Trinitarian contemplations regarding the creation of Adam.

> Then God said, "Let us make man in our image, after our likeness."

The roots of our present-day experience of loneliness are all found here. Notice the pronouns. "Then God [singular] said, 'Let us [plural] make man in our [plural] image.'" This is Trinitarian theology, the very first in Scripture. It hints at the singular nature of God and the plurality of persons within the Godhead. Scripture unveils this further in Deuteronomy 6:4, "Hear, O Israel: the LORD our God, the LORD is one." Some have described it as the John 3:16 of Judaism. Every service in a Jewish synagogue begins with these words, and faithful Jews quote them daily. The oneness of God is also a fundamental truth in Christianity.

On the surface it might not be apparent how this relates to loneliness, yet the essence of our loneliness is rooted in Trinitarian theology. Let's spend a little time in the deep end of the theology pool.

ONE IN NUMBER

How is God one? The oneness of God in number (monotheism) is the most obvious implication of the verse, also known as monotheism. Some verses in Scripture do seem to imply that there are other gods.[5] However, these verses are not saying there actually are other gods; instead, they call for Israel to worship the One true God rather than the make-believe gods of the pagan world. God is not the best choice or the first of many gods; He is the One and only.

ONE IN UNITY/SIMPLICITY

Here, God's oneness takes us to the deep end of the doctrinal pool and points out an unintended error many Christians have in their view of God. Theologians call this the *simplicity of God*. That is not to say there is anything intellectually simple about God or that this concept is simple. Instead, the essence of God's being is simple. He is a singularity. He is an absolute unity of oneness. The classic definition is that God is not made up of any parts. Everything about God, and in God, is God.

Many people think about God and don't think about His essence but aggregate His attributes. God is love. God is spirit. God is power. Here is the danger: We can think about God as we think about a recipe where God is a dash of this and a cup of that, and you mix it up, and out of the oven comes God. We easily compartmentalize God according to the attributes we prefer. When I was in seminary, I remember making this mistake on a paper or two. My professors went ballistic. I was failing on the simplicity of God because it is so easy to do.

God is not part this or part that. He is not merely "attribute this" and "attribute that." When we do that, we deify the attribute itself, diminishing the actual God. The most common example of this is the love of God. Humans like love, and we quickly reduce God to this single attribute. Yes, He is love, but He is simple, a singularity.

Remember, all that God is, is God. His love is a holy love. His mercy is a just mercy, and His justice is a merciful justice. His power is a wise power. He is not a part; He is a whole, a unity. He is one. Article 1 of the famous Belgic Confession (1561) begins with: "That there is one only simple and spiritual Being, which we call God."[6] This historic confession of doctrine starts with the principle of the simplicity of God. It is that important.

UNITY IN DIVERSITY

If you come from a church background, you may be wondering how God is a unity if He is also triune. Here is the marvel of God's essence. He is an absolute singularity, *and* He is a diversity. This sounds like double talk. The Lord is one, *and* the Lord is three. We call it the Trinity. Tri (three). Unity (one). The Old Testament hints at this—the Spirit hovering over the waters in creation, the fourth man in Daniel's fiery furnace, messianic prophecies with an eternal throne. What is veiled in the Old Testament is revealed in the New Testament. There are many examples of the Trinity in the New Testament, such as the Spirit conceiving Jesus in His mother, Mary, and the Father's words and Spirit's dovelike appearance at Jesus' baptism. None makes it more evident than Jesus' commission in Matthew 28:19, "Go therefore and make disciples of all nations, baptizing them in the name of the Father and of the Son and of the Holy Spirit."

In what can only be described as a mystery, the singularity of God includes three distinct persons. There is only one God. Yet God is also an "us." A plurality. A community. God is a mysterious, simultaneous Oneness and Threeness. The emphasis in the Gospels is much more than the corporate organizational chart of God. It is the deep love between the Father, Son, and Spirit (theologians call this "perichoresis"). Their mutual passion is so abiding, eternal, and covenantal that the three are eternally one.

WHY DO I FEEL SUCH PROFOUND LONELINESS?

The story of human loneliness has its roots in the character of God and God's purpose in creating us.

> So God created man in his own image, in the image of God he created him; male and female he created them. And God blessed them. (Gen. 1:27–28)

The roots of our present-day experience of loneliness are all found right here. We were made in the likeness of a relational, communicating, and triune God. His social nature is hardwired into our nature. We were designed for relational fulfillment vertically with God and horizontally with other humans. Like God, these relationships are fulfilling by design to the extent that they are harmonious. God's threeness is the paradigm for our social needs, and His oneness is the paradigm for human relationships marked by love and peace.

You know, like the old song says: "you don't know what you've got till it's gone."[7] Loneliness is first theological before it is existential. Loneliness isn't the opposite of relational fulfillment. It is the absence of it. Loneliness is an experiential void and vacuum. Its pain is a backhanded compliment to the pleasure of what God originally designed.

We are on a crucial truth that I urge you to consider carefully. I know this is hard, as I have had seasons where I was drowning in loneliness. Ask God to renew your mind so that you may think differently about your loneliness. Our feelings generally flow from our knowings, at least what we believe is true about loneliness. Lou Priolo connects these dots:

GOD'S THREENESS IS THE PARADIGM FOR OUR SOCIAL NEEDS, AND HIS ONENESS IS THE PARADIGM FOR HUMAN RELATIONSHIPS MARKED BY LOVE AND PEACE.

> You see, in order to change your feelings, you have to change your thoughts as well as your actions. So, I would like to suggest (as have others) that loneliness starts as a state of mind before it becomes a feeling. The way you think about being alone affects the way you feel about it. If, for example, you believe that to avoid being lonely you must always have another human being at your side, you are likely to be a very lonely person indeed.[8]

The depth of your loneliness signals the opposite height of your potential joy. Think of it like a swing. My young daughters love to swing and love me to push them as they swing. The higher, the better. I do a run-under to get them as high as possible. They squeal in delight as they swing to the opposite side equally high.

Let's be honest. Loneliness pain is acute. It can be overwhelming. Debilitating. Even life-threatening. Yet the pain can be part of the cure if we understand the pain like a swing; the greater the pain, the greater the potential pleasure. God made us to feel emotionally the absence of the presence of His purpose. I am convinced this is why we feel lonely in the manner we do.

In this way, loneliness is a gift from God. It is intended to prod us toward what is best for us. This is God's grace, and it applies both vertically and horizontally. The absence of a reconciled relationship with our Creator is spiritual pain, and the lack of meaningful relationships with others is social pain.

And the story of loneliness emerges in a garden.

Discussion Questions

1) How does the book of Genesis help your understanding of loneliness?

2) The author writes, "God's threeness is the paradigm for our social needs, and His oneness is the paradigm for human relationships marked by love and peace." How can you emulate God's threeness and oneness in your relationships?

3) The focus of this book is viewing loneliness spiritually. How have you connected loneliness with your faith journey so far? How would you describe loneliness in spiritual terms?

Alone, Not Lonely

FAMILY OF ORIGIN. One's family of origin explains a lot in counseling and therapy circles. As much as we may want to escape the patterns of dysfunction we observed in our childhood, they impress much upon our souls. Our family of origin largely shapes our formation as people.

The Bible gives a detailed portrait of our family of origin, and it's not pretty. It starts wonderfully and is full of promise. Genesis 2 provides a detailed account of God creating the first human, Adam. He was made from the dust of the ground. God breathed His own life into Adam, and humanity began as a unique species in creation. There was a beautiful garden for Adam to tend. He had tasks like naming the animals. It was an earthly paradise that provided for all his physical needs. Adam was in harmony with God and with his environment. The vertical dimension of his *imago Dei* was perfect and flourishing.

Yet something was missing. Adam had no horizontal reflection of the social Trinity. There was a he but no she. The divine reflection was incomplete, as Adam had no equal with whom to share a loving relationship. This led God to one final stroke in His creation masterpiece.

ALONE

"Then the LORD God said, 'It is not good that the man should be alone; I will make him a helper fit for him'" (Gen. 2:18). God views Adam's aloneness as "not good." The traditional interpretation, as heard at many a wedding, goes something like this: "God looked down and saw a he-pheasant and a she-pheasant, and a she-rhino and a he-rhino, but for Adam, there was no counterpart, so God made Eve." This is an accurate statement. However, the insinuation is that God was fixing Adam's problem, which was that he was a bachelor. This is inherently "not good."

This misses the larger picture in two ways. First, God's assessment of "not good" is first theological. Remember, God's purpose in creating humanity was that we would uniquely reflect what God is like. God assesses Adam's aloneness as an insufficient divine reflection. The word in Hebrew for "good" is *tov*. It is the same word used later when God assesses His entire creation and calls it "very good." The word means morally and aesthetically excellent. It is as if God is His own artistic critic, who steps back from the grandeur of creation and, with a perfect eye for beauty, declares all of it glorious.

Yet, Adam being alone, God said, is less than what is most excellent. His creation of Eve completes the social reflection of God's tri-unity. Like God, humanity is now a plurality of equals; Adam as male, and Eve as female. Both are full image bearers who, together, are a context of communication, love, admiration, and delight, similar to how God the Father, Son, and Spirit relate to each other.

The second implication speaks to the many people who view singles and their singleness as a problem to be solved. I know this well as I was a single pastor for twenty years. I grew accustomed to that awkward moment after church services when well-intentioned people would introduce me to their single nieces, cousins, and friends. They often told me later that this particular bachelorette "needed somebody like me in their life." Just what I was looking for, a project wife. I remember one time I was visiting former members of our church who had moved to another state. We had lunch together in their home. Their six-year-old daughter looked at me and whispered to her mom, "Is he married?" The mom replied, "No." The little girl proclaimed loudly for all to hear, "That's odd."

There is an unfortunate ethos in evangelical churches in which people mistake aloneness for loneliness. They often go together, but marriage is a solution to one, not necessarily to the other. There will be more on this later, but it applies to this point. Single Christians may sense whispers around them. "That's odd." No, it's not. Half the adult American population is single. Many of the heroes of the early church were single. And perhaps most importantly, Jesus was unmarried. Single adults are not odd. They are alone maritally, just like Adam and Jesus were.

LEARNING THE DISTINCTIONS BETWEEN LONELINESS, ALONENESS, AND SOLITUDE IS ESSENTIAL TO UNDERSTANDING WHAT IS UNDESIRABLE (LONELINESS), NEUTRAL (ALONENESS), AND GOOD (SOLITUDE).

Please note that God doesn't say it is not good that Adam is lonely (although that is true). Eve wasn't provided to fix Adam's loneliness. He was a complete human in a beautiful garden in complete harmony with his Creator. Adam didn't need a wife for his loneliness; she was a provision for his aloneness. Learning the distinctions between loneliness, aloneness, and solitude is essential to understanding what is undesirable (loneliness), neutral (aloneness), and good (solitude). Paul Tillich notes that "our language has wisely sensed those two sides of being alone. It has created the word 'loneliness' to express the pain of being alone. And it has created the word 'solitude' to express the glory of being alone."[1] June Hunt describes solitude as aloneness by choice and loneliness as aloneness, not by choice.[2] The former is a blessing, the latter a pain. We aim to understand how to turn our unchosen loneliness into mere aloneness and our aloneness into enriching solitude.

If you interviewed Adam before Eve's arrival and asked him, "Adam, so, you got it pretty good here. Eden produces all you need to eat or drink. You've named every animal, and they like you. Your bachelor pad is a lush garden. Yet, inquiring minds want to know, you must notice that there are he-pheasants and she-pheasants, he-rhinos and she-rhinos. Does it make you lonely?" He would have said, "What is this 'lonely' you speak of? I walk every day with God." Adam was horizontally alone. There is no necessary correlation between being single and lonely, nor is there one between being married and not lonely. Eve was a gracious gift from God to complement Adam's maleness and the life-complement to Adam's aloneness, summarized in the words "helper fit" (Gen. 2:18). She was a wonderful gift to help Adam (and for Adam to help her) and to mate, which was necessary to fulfill the creation mandate to fill and subdue the earth. Hence, God calls her a "helper fit," which in some ways, Adam was to Eve as well.

NAKEDNESS AND LONELINESS

While the story thus far explains aloneness, we have yet to uncover loneliness' painful entrance. At the end of Genesis 2, Adam's life is human perfection, perfect harmony with God, and perfect harmony with his wife, Eve. Similarly, Eve is the most satisfied woman and wife ever. Neither of them is alone horizontally or vertically. They are the most non-lonely, relationally flourishing humans ever. If only the story of loneliness had stopped there.

I'd encourage you to read Genesis 3, as it tells of Adam and Eve's willful choice to disobey God. The immediate consequences are enlightening, as aloneness reenters the story and loneliness tragically appears as well.

> Then the eyes of both were opened, and they knew that they were naked.
>
> And they sewed fig leaves together and made themselves loincloths. And they heard the sound of the LORD God walking in the garden in the cool of the day, and the man and his wife hid themselves from the presence of the LORD God among the trees of the garden. But the LORD God called to the man and said to him, "Where are you?" And he said, "I heard the sound of you in the garden, and I was afraid, because I was naked, and I hid myself." He said, "Who told you that you were naked? Have you eaten of the tree of which I commanded you not to eat?" (Gen. 3:7–11)

Where does loneliness come from? Sin created loneliness. This passage doesn't say "lonely," as the emphasis here is not Adam's loneliness but Adam's nakedness. Before sin, Adam and Eve didn't wear clothing, just like all the created animals. But Adam and Eve feel physical shame for their moral corruption. Consider God's question, "Who told you that you were naked?" What's the answer? No one. Nakedness is not essentially the absence of clothing (in a certain sense, it is). Nakedness is the absence of righteousness. It is first a spiritual condition before God. We all know the feeling of nakedness. I don't think I need to describe it here.

Have you considered that nakedness only feels like nakedness when someone else is around? In this way, nakedness begins as a spiritual reality but ends as a social one. Most of us bathe or shower naked daily without thinking too much about it. But in a public setting, it's a different story. Why? The answer has everything to do with the causes of loneliness. Nakedness is what sinners feel when spiritually exposed before God and socially exposed before others. Even in our secular culture, nudists are scandalous.

What is this all about? It goes back to Genesis: "Then God said, 'Let us make man in our image.'" We were made for total vulnerability before God and others. Sin has shattered us right down to our core nature. The result is that we are spiritually separated from God and socially distanced from one another. Without the gospel, we are now and forever alienated from our Creator. What should we call the pervasive and enduring ache such vertical and horizontal distance creates within us? What word should we apply to the sense that someone and something is missing? The word in English is *loneliness*.

Tracing our longings backward to a not-yet-achieved satisfaction is insightful. C. S. Lewis did the same when he wrote,

Creatures are not born with desires unless satisfaction for those desires exists. A baby feels hunger; well, there is such a thing as food. A duckling wants to swim; well, there is such a thing as water. Men feel sexual desire; well, there is such a thing as sex. If I find in myself a desire which no experience in this world can satisfy, the most probable explanation is that I was made for another world.[3]

God made clothes for Adam and Eve. Our need for clothing has little to do with the weather, although as a guy who lives through Chicago winters, I'm glad for thick clothing. In the story of loneliness, clothes are simply fashionable hiding. Clothes hide the most personal parts of our bodies. They are barriers between who we are and who we hope people see us to be. They are emblematic of the social barriers we both hate and desperately need, lest people discover who we truly are.

LONELINESS AS EDENIC WRECKAGE

While clothing hides us from humans, it doesn't hide us from God. We are morally naked before a God who "tests our hearts" (1 Thess. 2:4). Romans 2:15 tells us that we all have a moral GPS "written on [our] hearts" that works with our conscience to affirm our guilt before God. What seized Adam and Eve one millisecond after they sinned? While the word in the text is "nakedness," the rest of the Bible explains nakedness as separation from God. Might we get to heaven and discover that our clothes closets were spiritual indicators of how much we miss God? How could we ignore it? Again, Romans explains,

> For although they knew God, they did not honor him as God or give thanks to him, but they became futile in their thinking, and their foolish hearts were darkened. Claiming to be wise,

they became fools. . . . Therefore God gave them up in the lusts
of their hearts to impurity, to the dishonoring of their bodies
among themselves, because they exchanged the truth about
God for a lie and worshiped and served the creature rather than
the Creator, who is blessed forever! Amen. (Rom. 1:21–25)

It turns out that nakedness needs a replacement god. Since we
can't be naked before a holy God, we substitute Him with less
convicting gods. Our secular age is filled with these replacement
gods and seeks to derive meaning and identity from them. The
apostle calls it all a lie. Isn't it interesting that modern people who
worship these counterfeit gods still wear clothes? Our preferable
gods cannot atone for the ancient guilt we still feel.

Loneliness acts as our relational conscience. As our moral conscience tells us when something is morally broken in us, loneliness tells us when something is relationally disordered. The ache
indicates the absence of what could fulfill us.

G. K. Chesterton had a gift for clever illustration. He com-
pares the modern person to a man (like Robinson Crusoe) who
washes up on the shore of an island.[4] He has amnesia due to the
trauma of what he just experienced. He looks around, and he
sees shards of wood on the sand. He observes wood planks and large torn fabric floating just offshore. He wonders what happened. While he can't remember exactly what happened, the remnants indicate that there once was a ship. He must have been on it, so he must be a sailor. The vessel must have once been whole and seaworthy.

THE STORY OF LONELINESS IS THE OVERARCHING STORY OF THE LOVELINESS OF CHRIST, WHO CAN AND WILL REMOVE OUR SHAME.

All of this can be safely surmised from the shattered remnants around him.

We live in a world of shards and planks. Clearly, something has gone desperately wrong. The wreckage indicates what we and this world once were. Nakedness and loneliness are Eden's spiritual debris and flotsam. We can extrapolate from their universal presence that it hasn't always been like this. Religion is humanity's attempt to make sense of the wreckage. Distance from God and awkward nakedness before others point to a time when we felt neither in the garden of Eden. We long to be in that garden again, without hiding or shame.

The gospel of Jesus provides this Edenic garden experience again. There is a cure to the vertical shame before God and our embarrassment before others. The story of loneliness is the overarching story of the loveliness of Christ, who can and will remove our shame. Are you ready to stop hiding?

Discussion Questions

1) How might the idea that there is a difference between alone and lonely change your perspective on loneliness?

2) As loneliness acts as our relational conscience, what words would describe what your conscience is saying?

3) If you were to trace your experience with loneliness as Edenic wreckage, what part of the perfect Eden would it indicate?

3

God's Purpose for Lonely Pain

IN THE HISTORY CHANNEL reality show *Alone*, contestants are put in remote locations in an endurance test. They are entirely alone (hence the name of the show). They must figure out how to survive. It is a physical test as the conditions are challenging. They must scavenge for food and shelter. They are not allowed any technology or contact with loved ones or the outside world. While the conditions are extreme, the real test is the separation from any other human being. The contestants compete against other contestants located near enough to share the conditions but far enough away not to allow communication. This is the competition: Who can live the longest without human interaction? The winner is awarded $1 million. Such is the gain for enduring relational pain.

One man who would easily win this was known as the loneliest man in the world. He lived in a Brazilian forest by himself from 1995 until his death in 2022.[1] He never spoke to anyone in the world outside his jungle. Until a recent sighting, only one blurry photo of him was proof that he existed. What must his life and longings have been like?

We humans don't like to be alone. For $1 million, we would consider it for a season. Otherwise, we need our people. Anyone who doesn't must be crazy. I read about one such person, St. Simeon Stylites the Elder. He lived during the turn of the fourth century. For apparently religious reasons, he was determined to live alone until he died. He built a pillar with a small platform on the top. The first pillar was nine feet tall. But he continued to build taller versions, the last over fifty feet tall. On that platform, he had no shelter, food, bed, or pillow. It was solitary confinement in the extreme. Locals and his disciples would bring him food. One can only imagine how he handled the other bodily needs and functions. Simeon stayed on that platform for thirty-six years.[2]

You will be happy to know you have not read this far only to have me suggest building a pillar and platform. I wish Simeon had read this book. He would have had much happier days! My goal is to reorient our thinking about the ache of loneliness, to turn it from a pain to be avoided into a kind of friend. This is how we avoid wasting it; indeed, we can use it in profoundly joy-giving ways. You may think, who needs a friend like loneliness? No, thank you. Unfortunately, the common ways people deal with loneliness waste its potential good.

HOW TO WASTE YOUR LONELINESS

Isolation

I am amazed as I drive around northern Michigan and its Upper Peninsula (I was born there!). It is beautiful. It is remote.

Tucked back away from the highway are many homes and trailers. As I pass them, I often wonder who these people are and how they make a go of it. Besides some nefarious deer hunting, the isolation is reminiscent of the History Channel's *Alone*. While some people thrive in such a setting, many isolate themselves due to painful human relationships. Proverbs captures this aspect of human nature: "Whoever isolates himself seeks his own desire; he breaks out against all sound judgment" (Prov. 18:1). This verse highlights that a terrible way to deal with loneliness is to move further away, to isolate more. Such is the irrational behavior of human beings.

We are inherently passive-aggressive. Each relational hurt we experience can push us deeper into the woods. While that may not be your mailing address, might it be your relational one? As people continue to disappoint us, we can become more and more reclusive. It is counterintuitive to cope with our desire for relational fullness by further withdrawing. Yet if it's not you, I'm confident you know people like this. They try to show how they don't care what people think of them by putting their heart deep in the woods, with fences, gates, German Shepherds, and scary signs warning of any trespassing. They won't talk to Mom and "don't care what she thinks." A deeper consideration of passive-aggressive human behavior reveals that isolating behavior shows how much, not how little, people are essential to us. The rejection indicates their high value; otherwise, why go to the isolation effort? Often what these people desperately want is to talk to Mom again. But the instinct to isolate solidifies and calcifies their loneliness.

Obsession

We all have desires in life, things we want to accomplish, or dimensions of life we hope to be fulfilled. We strive for them, long for them, and labor for them. And all too often, they don't become a reality in our lives. And even when they do, frequently they aren't quite what we hoped they would be. When these are unmet relational longings, there are daily reminders of who or what isn't there. If you have gone through a divorce, or the death of a spouse or family member, these reminders are inescapable: children, holidays, family photos, finances, weddings, funerals, graduations, daily chores, etc. It regularly feels like there's an empty chair at the dinner table.

In my own story, I struggled greatly with my desire for family life during my alone years. Each night I came home, everything was exactly as it was when I left. There was never a surprise, never a difference. I used to say the only thing worse than lots of noise in the house was no noise in the house. The utter predictability and quiet of my alone life stirred my growing resentment. It is like the game you play with kids where you challenge them not to think about something. The process of not thinking about it only makes you think about it more.

Unmet desires can easily lead us to obsessive and destructive behavior. One woman describes her coping this way:

> Believing that I should not have to live with unfulfilled long-ings, I got what I wanted when I wanted it. Clothes, trips to Europe, or weekends away—put on credit cards or financed some way, until I had approximately $7,000-$10,000 debt by the time I was twenty-two. The other thing I desired and felt like I needed now was a man—consequently, I would date men I was not even interested in or men that I knew only wanted to sleep with me. To have dates, I would occasionally go ahead and have sex just to feel accepted.[3]

Her testimony echoes that of the Preacher in Ecclesiastes.

> And whatever my eyes desired I did not keep from them. I kept my heart from no pleasure, for my heart found pleasure in all my toil, and this was my reward for all my toil. Then I considered all that my hands had done and the toil I had expended in doing it, and behold, all was vanity and a striving after wind, and there was nothing to be gained under the sun. (Eccl. 2:10–11)

These longings are not themselves sinful when we desire to fulfill them according to God's will. Yet our desires are easily amplified into obsessions, good desires weaponized against us. When our "like to have" becomes "lust to have" or "must have," chaos will ensue. Our lives and thinking become disordered and dangerous. A reality check awaits. Either we will collapse as the longing remains unfulfilled or be devastated when the longing is fulfilled but fails to satisfy (as Ecclesiastes emphasizes).

A coming chapter deals with contentment when life isn't what we want. Here I urge you to surrender your must-have list to God. Healthy loneliness keeps God as the bottom line of your must-have list. As Augustine noted, your restless heart will remain so until it truly is satisfied in Him.

How? Here are some helpful diagnostic questions to apply to your unmet expectations.

EITHER WE WILL COLLAPSE AS THE LONGING REMAINS UNFULFILLED OR BE DEVASTATED WHEN THE LONGING IS FULFILLED BUT FAILS TO SATISFY (AS ECCLESIASTES EMPHASIZES).

- *Is this a desire consistent with God's will for my life?*
- *If I were to do what I desire, would God be pleased?*
- *Am I fully committed to only fulfilling this desire within God's will?*
- *How can I glorify God if this desire is never realized in my life?*

Loneliness indicates some level of unfulfilled desires in life. Loneliness will bless our lives only if loneliness remains loneliness. Once loneliness weaponizes, it turns predatory and destructive. How do we de-escalate obsessive loneliness? Listen to our Savior's tender invitation: "Come to me, all who labor and are heavy laden, and I will give you rest" (Matt. 11:28). Since knowing Jesus is the one true ultimate satisfaction for our souls, His care for our laden and lonely hearts tempers our desperation.

I am convinced this is a primary purpose for loneliness, to keep turning our souls toward God. How else will sinners arrive at the conclusion, "Whom have I in heaven but you? And there is nothing on earth that I desire besides you. My flesh and my heart may fail, but God is the strength of my heart and my portion forever" (Ps. 73:25–26). If we deal with loneliness in a healthy way, we will arrive at the conclusion that only God is the strength and satisfaction of our hearts. Obsessive loneliness eats itself and wastes the pricks and prods of unmet expectations.

Distraction

Blaise Pascal, the famous French mathematician and theologian from the seventeenth century, thought deeply about these things. One of his more famous statements is this one: "I have discovered that all the unhappiness of men arises from one single fact, that they cannot stay quietly in their own chamber."[4] Not much has changed in three hundred years, except the distractions have greatly multiplied. Entertainment is available to fill all the moments that might otherwise provide time for relationship building. Such are the strange and lonely days we live in.

A look in any restaurant these days will show another reality. A family sitting around a table for a meal. What are they all doing? Talking? Sharing? Laughing? No. They are all on their phones (and not likely reading their Bibles or great works of literature on them). They are scrolling, searching, and hoping for a low-level dopamine hit from something interesting or new.

The average person checks their phone 344 times per day, once every four minutes.[5] Each glance is a fleeting hope that someone acknowledged them with a like or comment, even as they largely ignore the embodied people around them. All that scrolling is a distraction from how God created us to live out our image bearing, namely, face-to-face human relationships and communication. In the words of one famous book, we are "amusing ourselves to death." Our amusements are keeping us from meaningful and life-giving relationships with God, others, and in a way, ourselves. There must be a better way.

HOW TO REDEEM LONELINESS

This book aims to diagnose loneliness biblically and prescribe gospel solutions to the relational ache. The Bible tells us why we feel this way. The gospel of Jesus empowers us to redeem our loneliness.

Embrace God's Purpose for Your Loneliness

Loneliness is part of the inner architecture of our image-bearing. It acts like sensors in our car to tell us when something is missing—oil in the engine or air in the tires. What do you do when the check engine oil light comes on? Ignore it? One of my college-aged sisters once called my dad and said, *My car isn't running anymore. I'm stuck on the highway.* My dad's whole career was as an engine engineer for John Deere. But his daughter never picked up that when the check engine oil light goes on, it's telling you something needs to be done.

For many people, that loneliness sensor has been flashing, and they keep driving. Loneliness isn't a sin; it's a sensor. In this way, it is a friend like a check engine oil light is a friend if we don't ignore it but use it to make healthy adjustments in our lives.

Loneliness is like hunger, thirst, or even our sex drive. God placed these longings in us to move us toward the things He graciously provided for our flourishing. None of these are exclusively Christian. Loneliness is part of God's common grace. When we are hungry, we work on getting food. When we are thirsty, we seek water. The discomfort spurs action and change.

Loneliness pain acts like rumble strips along the road. I like to drive those occasionally to annoy my family, but when you hear that *brrrr*, what do you think? I'm off the road. I'd better course correct. When you feel lonely, think *brrrr*. I need a course correction in my life.

Allow Loneliness Pain to Motivate You

We are far from the first people group to detest loneliness. The Bible includes people experiencing profound loneliness.

"All my intimate friends abhor me, and those whom I loved have turned against me." (Job 19:19)

The heart knows its own bitterness, and no stranger shares its joy. (Prov. 14:10)

"My God, my God, why have you forsaken me?" (Matt. 27:46)

As these verses indicate, loneliness hurts. It hurts bad. Yet God embedded these prickly emotional reminders of how wonderful harmony with God and others can be. The pain is a measure of the loss. Not all pain is bad. Loneliness pain comes to us ethically neutral. What we do with it determines whether it is good or bad pain. When I work out, the muscle pain tells me I'm doing something good for me. It's a good pain if I let it motivate me to further effort. That's the goal of loneliness. Turn it into good pain. Our natural response is to make loneliness pain "bad" and then make the cause of the pain worse. Before you know it, you are building a cabin in the Upper Peninsula as a monument to your loneliness. When loneliness spirals downward, it dehumanizes and increases our pain.

Loneliness is our relational conscience. It tells us when something isn't healthy or as healthy as possible. Or, like nerves in the body that indicate we are touching something too hot or too cold, the nerves are fulfilling their intended purpose. God put in us a relational nervous system. Emotional discomfort is loneliness doing its job.

I recently had a mild bout with shingles. Shingles are when nerve endings are enflamed and extra sensitive to touch. Depressive loneliness is the acute pain we feel when our loneliness is inflamed. This may have led you to read this book. You may have

recently suffered a relational loss or disappointment. Your loneliness is at the shingles stage; enflamed, extremely sensitive, and
burning. No vaccine protects us from the acute level of loneliness. But the gospel of Jesus provides soothing balm and redemptive cream to relieve our pain. In His own words, "a bruised reed
he will not break, and a smoldering wick he will not snuff out"
(Matt. 12:20 NIV). These represent two extremely fragile objects,
yet not too fragile for our Savior's tender touch.

Before our loneliness turns acute, we need the regular practice
of healthy loneliness. Golf teaches so many life lessons, and here
is a key one: a lousy shot must be quickly forgotten. The pros
are good at it. Amateurs are not. Since golf is so mental, a bad
shot quickly turns into five, as each one takes your mental attitude down with it. Loneliness has a compounding quality, both
negative and positive. In all my years of aloneness and loneliness,
few things helped more than the discipline of taking the pain and
wrestling with it in my emotions to turn it positive.

That is more easily said than done. As you read this, my heart is
for you, and this may seem too overwhelming to gain emotional
mastery over it. As a guy who has been there, I won't claim anything near a perfect record. Are there still holidays where being
alone is suffocating? Yes. Can you apply every principle in this
book and still struggle when others seem internally healthy and
happy? Again, yes. I still do.

Since loneliness is not a sin but a struggle, I believe God delights
in our uneven attempts to overcome loneliness with the gospel,
faith, and hope. It reminds me of a story about a famous composer
who wrote a very difficult score for the violin. One of the most
talented violinists available agreed to play the piece. She practiced
and practiced, but it proved too difficult. She finally went to the

composer and said, "What you have written is too challenging to play. I must give up." The composer said, "No. You see, what I'm looking for in the piece is the sound of someone trying to play it."

Too often, we are harder on ourselves than God is. Remember, "he knows our frame; he remembers that we are dust" (Ps. 103:14). The pain of loneliness is in our emotional architecture by God's design. He is honored as we try to "play what He composed" in us.

Determine to View Loneliness as a Gift

It doesn't feel like a gift, and most of us would prefer not to receive it. Yet, there it is daily, staring us in the face. Might this be a "daily bread" prayer to God? What if we asked Him for the grace to choose to view loneliness as a gift from Him?

You may say, *but I don't like the feeling of loneliness*! I agree. But do you like the feeling of hunger or thirst? We generally don't want them, but we are thankful for them. While uncomfortable, they urge us toward what we need. If someone has no appetite or a sense of dehydration, that person is in a health crisis. Hunger and thirst cause us to seek the satisfaction of those desires. Loneliness is relational hunger. It sits in the pit of our souls uncomfortably. We can ignore it, distract it, satisfy it sinfully, resent it, or hate it. The key is to leverage it by seeing it as a gift and responding to it rightly.

WE CAN IGNORE IT, DISTRACT IT, SATISFY IT SINFULLY, RESENT IT, OR HATE IT. THE KEY IS TO LEVERAGE IT BY SEEING IT AS A GIFT AND RESPONDING TO IT RIGHTLY.

What does that look like? Loneliness creates internal energy. It is a strong emotion. I respond to it negatively, and even sinfully, by coping with the pain in sinful or destructive ways. Or I can leverage that energy as motivation toward a more profound engagement with God and others. This requires discipline and self-control as my flesh urges self-destructive responses.

The United States continues to suffer from incidents of mass shootings and murder. After the event, authorities investigate why the shooters do such terrible evil. The common denominator of most mass shooters is that they are loners. Their alienation from relationships that would be life-giving to them causes them to take loneliness energy and use it tragically and destructively.

Christian theology explains "why" our internal desires so easily weaponize loneliness.

"But I say, walk by the Spirit, and you will not gratify the desires of the flesh. For the desires of the flesh are against the Spirit, and the desires of the Spirit are against the flesh, for these are opposed to each other, to keep you from doing the things you want to do" (Gal. 5:16–17).

The flesh is our remaining nature, our "indwelling sin." It is a lingering spiritual enemy within that seizes upon any opportunity, temptation, or habit of life and weaponizes it against us and God's good purpose in us. It is critical to understand how our internal enemy works. Our flesh is an active force seeking our spiritual pain and sorrow. It hates God and will apprehend the slightest prick of loneliness and seek to amplify it into bitterness, jealousy, and resentment.

Once loneliness enters the lower side of our nature, viewing it as a gift is very difficult as it produces the worst of human emotions. Embedded in unhealthy loneliness is the fear that we will always feel this way. Just as hunger can devolve into gluttony and thirst weaponized into alcoholism, loneliness is easily weaponized within us.

Pascal rewinds loneliness to its source:

> What is it then that this desire and this inability proclaim to us, but that there was once in man a true happiness of which there now remain to him only the mark and empty trace, which he in vain tries to fill from all his surroundings, seeking from things absent the help he does not obtain in things present? But these are all inadequate, because the infinite abyss can only be filled by an infinite and immutable object, that is to say, only by God Himself.[6]

What Pascal describes as a hole in our heart, Augustine famously said, "Our heart is restless until it rests in you."[7] If this chapter discourages you, realize the natural you, by yourself, cannot turn loneliness into a blessing. It is always a curse and a scourge. For some, they isolate themselves in the wilderness, literally or figuratively. Others take their hurt out in violent and tragic ways.

The story of humanity is how much the hole in the heart hurts. How can we fill it? How can we find Augustine's rest? The tale of loneliness is intertwined with the story of redemption. The gospel is God's ultimate solution to our loneliness.

Discussion Questions

1) This chapter outlines three ways we can waste our loneliness: *isolation, obsession,* and *distraction*. Which of these traps are you most prone to fall into? What traps would you add to this list?

2) The author discusses three ways we can redeem loneliness: *embracing God's purpose for our loneliness, allowing loneliness-pain to motivate you,* and *determining to view loneliness as a gift*. Which of these ways do you find easiest to embrace? Which do you find most challenging?

3) Does your loneliness feel permanent to you? How? Why? What parts of the redemptive story encourage you that your struggle with loneliness can improve?

Gospelize Your Loneliness

CONSIDER ALL THE DIVERSE WAYS people try to cope with their loneliness. A partial list would include: medicating it, sexualizing it, ignoring it, obsessing over it, hating it, denying it, therapy it, party it, and even self-harm because of it. Each offers some relief, but they don't resolve it because they don't address the core causes.

As we saw earlier, we are lonely because of sin, but loneliness is not itself a sin. It is a powerful indication that we are made for relational harmony vertically with God and horizontally with others. Humans can enjoy deep and meaningful relationships with other humans without the gospel. These relationships provide some of what we long for but cannot resolve our core loneliness.

We are first and foremost lonely for God, our Creator. This vertical dimension of loneliness highlights our primary created purpose, and without it, even the best human relationships leave us with a strong sense that something is missing. But with a genuine relationship with God, we don't look to others to satisfy what only God can provide.

Jesus implicitly highlights this with a simple yet profound statement in John 16. This is part of Jesus' Upper Room teaching. It is a kind of final will and testament, since within roughly eighteen hours, Jesus will be dead on the cross. As the Son of God, He knew the details of His coming suffering. He tells His disciples in John 16:32, "Behold, the hour is coming, indeed it has come, when you will be scattered, each to his own home, and will leave me alone. Yet I am not alone, for the Father is with me."

WE SEE HOW JESUS GOES VERTICAL WHEN THE HORIZONTAL HAS HURT AND DISAPPOINTED HIM.

Jesus prophesies that His closest friends will all abandon Him. They did this in the garden of Gethsemane when Judas arrived with the Pharisees and soldiers to arrest Jesus. Has a trusted person in your life abandoned you? How about your top twelve? Such was Jesus' experience. Yet Jesus says that despite His core team leaving Him, He knows He is not alone because God the Father is always with Him. His vertical relationship with God the Father was sufficient for Him, even when His closest human relationships were shattered.

Do you see your loneliness in Jesus' way? How would you respond, as painful as it is to consider, if your most treasured friends left you? We see how Jesus goes vertical when the horizontal has hurt and disappointed Him.

The organizing principle of this book is that the gospel of Jesus restores us to our Creator God and provides a pattern to follow of love (which diminishes loneliness) and community with others (which enhances belonging). If you take the horizontal suggestions to heart without reconciliation with God by faith in Jesus, you will continue to feel lonely for the most important One your heart longs for, God Himself.

BY THE GOSPEL ⟶ *RECONCILE WITH GOD*

You often hear people citing the reason for their relational breach as "irreconcilable differences." They typically mean by this that the relational issues are so gnarled that no amount of trying can untangle the relationship. Pascal's "hole in the heart" and Augustine's "restless heart" describe what Adam and Eve lost in the garden. Yes, they lost their moral innocence and their marital harmony.

> **LONELINESS IS WHAT IMAGE BEARERS FEEL WHEN SOMETHING OR SOMEONE WE WERE MADE TO LIVE FOR IS ABSENT.**

But by far the most significant loss was that they lost God. All the other losses resulted from the infinite abyss now separating them from the One their soul was designed to know, treasure, and worship.

Loneliness is what image bearers feel when something or someone we were made to live for is absent. The restoration of this Person means the mitigation of His absence. At the center of the gospel of Christianity is precisely this restoration via reconciliation with God. Sin created the breach. Repentance and faith in Christ restore us to God and, importantly for loneliness, God to us. The apostle Paul describes the gospel in terms of reconciliation:

> and through him to reconcile to himself all things, whether on earth or in heaven, making peace by the blood of his cross.
> And you, who once were alienated and hostile in mind, doing evil deeds, he has now reconciled in his body of flesh

by his death, in order to present you holy and blameless and above reproach before him. (Col. 1:20–22)

Apart from this reconciliation, our condition before God is "alienation," "hostility," and the absence of objective peace with a holy God. Sin stole God from us. Jesus' cross can restore God to us. Through Christ, we are eternally reconciled to God. The "hole in our heart" is filled when we trust in Jesus as our Lord and Savior. God is ours forevermore.

Most people think about their loneliness in strictly horizontal terms. "If so-and-so didn't reject me, I wouldn't feel this way." Or "If I had a best friend, spouse, child, grandma, or a decent bowling team in my life, I wouldn't feel this way." While all these relationships are valuable, if you have all of them but don't reconcile with your Creator, the loneliness of the soul remains.

We were made for much more than any horizontal relationship can provide. We were magnificently made for God, and we will never find lasting peace and diminished loneliness until we are spiritually restored to Him. Without this first step, all the others are only temporary bits of help for loneliness. It starts with God. Be reconciled to Him. Repent of your sins. Trust in Jesus as your Lord and Savior. It is the foundation of redeeming our loneliness.

FROM THE GOSPEL → *DEATH TO SELF*

This is both the most critical and complex step to overcoming loneliness. Becoming a true Christian means surrendering all our attempts at self-salvation. Within the DNA of saving faith is humility, as it requires a dying-to-self to trust in Jesus fully. If it's anything less than that, it's not the kind of faith that saves us in God's assessment. This surrender to self is spiritual humility the gospel requires for every sinner.

Jesus describes this in even more graphic terms: death to self. "If anyone would come after me, let him deny himself and take up his cross and follow me. For whoever would save his life will lose it, but whoever loses his life for my sake will find it" (Matt. 16:24–25).

This is more than a clever turn of the phrase. Jesus is describing a cause and effect. At a minimum, to be a Christian is to deny myself. Essentially, I displace "me" from the throne of my heart. I remove the agenda of self from the top of my priority list and as the functional god of my life. By God's grace, Christ is enthroned in me and over me. I want His kingdom to come and His will to be done. God's agenda over mine is described as a crucified life. "I have been crucified with Christ. It is no longer I who live, but Christ who lives in me" (Gal. 2:20). Jesus clarifies this further in Matthew 16:25 and explains the effect of self-denial: "For whoever would save his life will lose it, but whoever loses his life for my sake will find it." Losing our life doesn't mean we physically die; instead, it means we surrender our self-agenda, self-exaltation, and self-worship. In my heart, *me* has been replaced by *He*. In this way, it is a kind of self-death.

On the surface, it sounds horrible, but Jesus promises whoever loses his life in this way actually gains his real and best life. One of my heroes in the faith, Jim Elliot, famously said it: "He is no fool who gives what he cannot keep to gain what he cannot lose."[1] This is paradoxical and a challenge to understand and apply. But if it were easy, it wouldn't require reading a book on loneliness, would it? According to Jesus, we kill loneliness by losing ourselves. We gain our full humanity by losing our old way of doing and feeling.

WITH THE GOSPEL ⟶ *BLESSED BY GIVING*

Often Christians view the gospel as a means to a blessed life and miss that it also provides us with a model. Jesus' life, ministry, and death offer us a living example of human flourishing. Following His pattern of life without genuine faith in Him is mere moralism. It may make us better people, but true power for transformed living is a heart changed by God and a life like His. Paul quotes Jesus to the Ephesian elders as a summary of the Christian life:

> "Remember the words of the Lord Jesus, how he himself said, 'It is more blessed to give than to receive.'" (Acts 20:35)

This verse is often quoted and applied to categories of stewardship and generosity. In reality, it applies everywhere to everything. When we displace our comfort and preferences and willingly inconvenience ourselves for the good and joy of others, we are blessed. Blessed is a rather broad term. To make it specific, blessed is a life with minimal loneliness and maximum meaning. I am urging you to fight your loneliness with the gospel. Gospelize your loneliness from the gospel, for the gospel, and with the gospel.

Gospelizing loneliness is precisely the opposite approach our instincts urge upon us. When we are lonely, we naturally ask, *Who can fill this void I feel? I need somebody to meet my needs!* I spent many years as a single Christian man living in the Christian singles scene, where this mentality is often displayed.

I remember years ago visiting a singles ministry event with the terrifying feeling only a single adult knows of walking into a room filled with people you don't know. I felt like I might as well be wearing a sign that says, "Hi, I'm Steve, and I'm needy." I remember that as the door closed behind me, everybody in the room stopped talking. The whole room paused, looked at me up and down, and then returned to their conversations. What happened in that moment? The assembled singles looked me over to see if I might be someone to meet their needs. Based on how quickly they returned to their conversations, the general assessment of the single women was no.

We can feel lonely in all kinds of human relationships: with parents, siblings, family, friends, spouse, in marital intimacy, casual and informal, close and intimate, spiritual, recreational, vocational, and others. The diversity of relationships we can enjoy (and long for) and the varying depth of intimacy we can sustain all complement the God whose relational image we bear.

THOSE WHO COME TO THE CHURCH LOOKING FOR PEOPLE OR THE CHURCH TO MEET THEIR NEEDS QUICKLY FLAME OUT.

I have spent over thirty years in church ministry. I have observed thousands of Christians pursuing relationships in a church community. The gospel paradox is repeated again and again. Those who come to the church looking for people or the church to meet their needs quickly flame out. In some ways, they are like me at the abovementioned singles gathering. They hope to meet people who will meet their needs. Or they expect the church to magically turn their lonely life into a fulfilled one. Their attitude in coming is, *I hope this church is filled with people ready to fulfill my desires!* They are looking to receive. Yet, Jesus said, blessing comes in giving, not receiving. Loneliness isn't diminished when we relationally take from people but when we relationally give. This explains why some people are constantly lonely in a local church (or constantly church shopping). Overcoming loneliness necessitates turning this approach upside down.

C. S. Lewis insightfully wrote,

The principle runs through all life from top to bottom. Give up yourself, and you will find your real self. Lose your life and you will save it. Submit to death, death of your ambitions and favourite wishes every day, and death of your whole body in the end: submit with every fibre of your being, and you will find eternal life. Keep back nothing. Nothing that you have not given away will be really yours. Nothing in you that has not died will ever be raised from the dead. Look for yourself, and you will find in the long run only hatred, loneliness, despair, rage, ruin, and decay. But look for Christ and you will find Him, and with Him everything else thrown in.[2]

Overcoming loneliness has little to do with gaining someone. We must lose someone. Who? Me. How? By giving myself to meet the relational and spiritual needs of others. This inversion of self is a profound transformation of the painful emotions of loneliness.

When we invert our natural desire to be loved and choose to love and serve others, the love of God *through* us mitigates the loneliness *in* us.

Self-giving love boomerangs back to us as a loneliness-killing blessing. To put it practically, if all your hopes for overcoming loneliness depend on someone to meet your relational needs, you will remain lonely. It is not the receiving of friendship but the giving of friendship that God intended for human flourishing. Essentially, we lose our loneliness by giving it away. We give it away by giving ourselves away.

I remember a riddle I heard as a kid: What gets wet as it dries?

Answer: a towel. It is a similar riddle we must resolve in our souls by determining to approach loneliness paradoxically. The more I try to meet the relational needs of others, the less lonely I feel. This is a zero-sum reality. My loneliness is directly proportional to the level of my selfishness. The more I delight in others *not* being lonely because of my investment in them, mysteriously, the less lonely I will feel.

Being a dad is one of the great marvels of my life and has taught me this lesson of love. I am astonished by the level of joy I get when my daughters enjoy something. In truth, I enjoy their experience of joy more than I enjoy my experience of joy. For example, when I die to my desire to go fishing and instead take them to the park, their giggles are better than catching a fish. When I set aside my to-do list and spontaneously say yes to their request for fun, my delight in their delight is greater than my delight in finishing my list. Whatever is sacrificed for the joy and happiness of others returns to us as the kind of joy Jesus called "blessed." This is what I call gospelizing our loneliness.

> **WHILE WE CAN'T ELIMINATE IT, LONELINESS DOESN'T HAVE TO DOMINATE US NOW, NOT IF WE LOSE OUR LIVES BY HELPING OTHERS FIND THEIRS.**

We will never be entirely rid of loneliness until heaven. Indeed, one of the terrifying things about hell is that it will be a constant, grinding aloneness, and maximum loneliness forever. But for Christians, eternity is loneliness-free forever. Our future is vertical and horizontal relational perfection. While we can't eliminate it, loneliness doesn't have to dominate us now, not if we lose our lives by helping others find theirs. Not if we lose our preferred life by helping others find theirs. Make this the habit of your life, and the love of God through you will diminish the loneliness in you. Try it. After a season of helping others, you will ask yourself, *Where did my loneliness go?*

Henri Nouwen's life story is complicated, but his brilliant insights into humanity's relational and spiritual needs are helpful. His struggles produced gems like this:

> When we feel lonely we have such a need to be liked and loved that we are hypersensitive to the many signals in our environment and easily become hostile toward anyone whom we perceive is rejecting us. . . . Once we have given up our desire to be fully fulfilled, we can offer emptiness to others. Once we have become poor, we can be a good host. . . . Poverty is the inner disposition that allows us to take away our defenses and convert our enemies into friends. We can perceive the stranger as an enemy only as long as we have something to defend. But when we say, "Please enter—my house is your house, my joy is your joy, my sadness is your sadness, and my life is your life," we have nothing to defend, since we have nothing to lose but all to give.[3]

Nouwen points out the necessary poverty of the soul that opens our lives and hearts to strangers, people in need, and often, surprising people who fill the void of our hearts. The gospel makes our hearts hospitable. How? Read on.

Discussion Questions

1) The author writes, "Those who come to the church looking for people or the church to meet their needs quickly flame out." Have you ever gone to a church looking for others to meet your needs?

2) This chapter states that "the love of God *through* us mitigates the loneliness *in* us." In your life, what is a practical way you can be a conduit of God's love (and consequently diminish your loneliness)?

3) "My loneliness is directly proportional to the level of my selfishness." How have you seen selfishness affect your sense of loneliness? How have you seen selflessness diminish your sense of loneliness?

Give the Love You Long For

A SIMPLE TRUTH LIES at the heart of this book and echoes the admonition of Jesus, "It is more blessed to give than to receive" (Acts 20:35). Human solutions to loneliness involve dulling the ache with social engagements, sexual encounters, social media, etc. These and many other apparent remedies leave the human heart longing for more. When our hope for curing loneliness is in receiving love, all human relationships prove disappointing. What is the opposite of this lonely receiving-love orientation? It is self-giving love. Self-giving love is where loneliness goes to die. As we saw earlier in the book, we must invert our natural desire to receive love by giving love. When we do, God's love through us alleviates our loneliness.

When were my darkest times of loneliness? While waves of dark loneliness could sweep over me at any time, they typically were when my sense of aloneness was heightened, often around the holidays or my birthday. Why? These are times of hopeful expectation of receiving attention, love, and gifts from family or friends. I guess I'm still a kid at heart. How easy it is for childhood expectations to become adult entitlements. I easily default to receive-love mode. When we do, loneliness gushes in. I think of the hundreds of thousands of elderly people in special care centers and nursing homes who receive professional care but little personal love. How difficult the days must be as they often have little receive-love. Our hearts certainly hurt for them.

SELF-GIVING LOVE IS WHERE LONELINESS GOES TO DIE.

As giving-love is the key to mitigating loneliness, in this chapter we will explore what kind of giving-love minimizes our loneliness. In short, it is Godlike love. It is Christlike love. The same love that pulsates through the Trinity, eternally satisfying their interpersonal desires, is the same kind of love God designed us to give away. By giving it, we enjoy what Jesus called in Acts 20:35 "blessed."

SELF-GIVING LOVE ALLEVIATES LONELINESS

Paul's magisterial letter to the Corinthian Christians reaches its zenith in chapter 13. The church of Corinth is a church that he planted and pastored for eighteen months. After he left, the church collapsed spiritually. Schisms of all different kinds beset them: people followed various leaders in the church, giving them allegiance that only Christ deserves; they were suing each other; they were sexually promiscuous with temple prostitutes, confused about marriage and singleness, haughty about Christian liberty issues, and were even perverting the Lord's Supper by turning it into a drinking party.

Ironically, their assessment of their spirituality was incredibly high. A primary reason was their possession of showy spiritual gifts (chapter 12). They failed to see that possessing spiritual gifts was no indication of spiritual maturity (the fruit of the Spirit is the indicator). Their basic orientation was toward themselves. The Corinthian church was a lonely church.

Chapter 13 is undoubtedly one of the most famous in all the Bible and for good reason. Theologian Adolf Harnack called this chapter "the greatest, strongest, deepest thing Paul ever wrote."[1] One writer warns, "Studying it is somewhat like taking apart a flower."[2] It is often read at weddings and special gatherings. This is part of our difficulty. It is so beautiful that it is easily turned into mere sentiment, like a Hallmark moment or some cheesy spiritual card. When we sentimentalize the grandeur of real love, it loses its force for calling us to live according to divine love. And without God's grace, none of us can. The ultimate expression of this love is not marriage or parenting or sexual love but a bloody Savior writhing in pain on an executioner's cross.

Read Paul's description of love carefully:

> Love is patient and kind; love does not envy or boast; it is
> not arrogant or rude. It does not insist on its own way; it is
> not irritable or resentful; it does not rejoice at wrongdoing,
> but rejoices with the truth. Love bears all things, believes all
> things, hopes all things, endures all things.
> Love never ends. (1 Cor. 13:4–8)

Despite this careful and famous definition, love is a most wonderful and misunderstood reality. We use the word for just about anything. We love our jeans, we love our dog, we love our school, we love ice cream, we love to water-ski, and we love to sleep in. Our English word "love" is so elastic that it doesn't mean much.

I remember lying in bed in my college dorm and listening as my roommate would whisper on the phone to some girl, *I love you.* Then a few days later, I'd hear him whisper to a different girl, *I love you.* What does love mean when offered in such a way? Is that love? The Corinthian church's problem was the same as our own. Their basic selfishness and pride closed their eyes to the fundamental nature of love—divine love, crucified love, and the expression of that love in Christian relationships. So, Paul gives them a description of real love in 1 Corinthians 13—ultimate love, real love.

Where Does Giving-Love Come From?

Secular evolutionists suggest love is a social construct, merely a function of evolutionary need. According to secularism, we need a male and female to reproduce; we need nurture and protection by parents; we need social love to protect the village. In other words, love is not a reality; it just appears to us to be.

The Bible answers this very differently. Love comes from God as God is love (1 John 4:8). Before God created, there was nothing but God. There was no universe, no heaven, and no angels. There was only God the Father, God the Son, and God the Spirit. Their relationship was eternally dynamic, filled with communication, joy, and laughter. They delighted in one another. God didn't create out of a need for more love. The Trinitarian relationships were enough. They were utterly non-lonely as the three persons of the Godhead derived their greatest joy in generating joy in the others. As an example, Jesus prays, "Father, I desire that they also, whom you have given me, may be with me where I am, to see my glory that you have given me because you loved me before the foundation of the world" (John 17:24).

What the Bible calls "love" is human etymology for the eternal self-relating within the Trinity, the delight and joy and self-giving for the good and enjoyment of the other. Love comes from God as God allows His creation (us) to participate in the energy of the Trinitarian relationships. When God created, He freely chose to build into human beings the capacity to relate to Him and one another as He relates to Himself. Human relationships picture the Trinitarian ones.

What do we see in the Trinity? Robust relating to others in self-giving. When we relate to one another in this way, we are participating in the reflective vibrancy of the life of the Trinity. Think about it. Why is love the greatest reality in the world? The very life of God humanly experienced in giving-love maximizes our joy as humans. Might this be why there are so many unhappy people today? Might this explain your unhappiness or loneliness today? People long to *be* loved, while true joy comes first from *giving* it.

What Does Giving-Love Look Like?

In short, God's love is displayed through Jesus on the cross. What did Jesus hold back? Nothing. What did He give? Everything. None of us can achieve such selflessness as our sinful nature continues to plague us. Yet the degree to which we provide and live for others is the same degree to which loneliness's ache diminishes. I often tell my church that if you are unsure what God would have you do,

THE DEGREE TO WHICH WE PROVIDE AND LIVE FOR OTHERS IS THE SAME DEGREE TO WHICH LONELINESS'S ACHE DIMINISHES.

consider what Satan would have you do, then do the opposite. In many ways, fighting loneliness is like that.

Our lonely actions are often reactions. These push relationships further away as the self seeks isolation and protection. Proverbs warns that he who isolates himself seeks his own desires (Prov. 18:1). Elijah was thinking about Elijah when he ran from Jezebel. Our instinct is self-love, and our natural tendency is away from the attitudes and actions that would heal relationships and soften loneliness.

New Testament scholar Leon Morris describes this love from 1 Corinthians 13 as

> a love for the utterly unworthy, a love that proceeds from a God who is love. It is a love lavished on others without a thought whether they are worthy or not. It proceeds from the nature of the lover, not from any attractiveness in the beloved. The Christian who has experienced God's love for him while he was yet a sinner (Rom. 5:8) has been transformed by the experience. Now he sees people as those for whom Christ died, the objects of God's love, and therefore the objects of the love of God's people. In his measure he comes to practise the love that seeks nothing for itself, but only the good of the loved one.[3]

It is a great irony that the cross displays both the greatest love and the greatest loneliness ever. Shortly before His death, Jesus' humanity shouted, "My God, my God, why have you forsaken me?" The answer was that God had placed upon His moral account our sin and guilt. There was a relational breach with Jesus' humanity that God's holiness required. This unique moment in human history shows what divine love is: a total surrender of self to God for the sake of others.

When waves of loneliness beset you, we should follow the paradigm of the cross. Look for someone for whom you can specifically inconvenience yourself to help. This shouldn't be too hard to accomplish as all around us are people in need. These needs may be material, physical, relational, or spiritual. All of them require our effort and sacrifice. Often, they are people we would not naturally be drawn toward. This is good, as a holy God is not naturally drawn toward sinners. We are vastly different than Him, yet He loved us. Love like that. Love like Him. His love is giving-love.

LONELINESS-KILLING LOVE IS STICKY

So much of my loneliness was and is self-inflicted. Relationships are too easily transactional, and when I'm not getting what I want, relationships can become disposable. Follow this pattern once, and it hurts. Follow it for decades, and your heart will dull toward people, both the ones you've known and the ones you could enjoy.

Paul highlights qualities of God's kind of love in 1 Corinthians 13: Love *bears all things, believes all things, hopes all things, endures all things*. Love *never ends*. I summarize these qualities of love with the word *sticky*. The meanings of the five clauses in this verse are slightly different.

Love "endures" all things is one of the Greek language's most illustrative words, and we see it in many other places in the New Testament. It is commonly translated *perseveres*. Here's why. It is a compound word. *Hupo* = under. *Meno* = to remain. *To remain under*. We are told to *hupomeno* in trials. We are to flee temptation but remain faithful in trials. Endure them. It is a stick-to-itiveness. Or stickiness. Love remains or endures under the pressure of life and relationships. In fact, for love, these pressures make it better, not worse. A helpful image may be that of a piece of carbon in the earth. Pressed by tons of pressure over time, it is refined and purified into a precious diamond. The carbon "hupo-menoed" and the weight pressure made it better and more beautiful.[4] Enduring love hangs in there with people. It can weather difficult circumstances.

The second description is a summary and sets up Paul's whole argument through chapter 14. Love never ends. It is also translated *love never fails*. The word means to *fall down*, as in love doesn't fall or quit. It is always up to the task. It always endures and never ends.

What does that mean regarding love's importance in the faith community of the church? We see where Paul is going in his argument, starting in verse 8: "As for prophecies, they will pass away; as for tongues, they will cease; as for knowledge, it will pass away." Spiritual gifts are great, but they are temporary. They will pass away. Love never passes away; it endures because God's love endures.

THE SOURCE OF LOVE'S ENDURANCE –
GOD'S ETERNAL NATURE

If we are honest, this is distressing because of what we see naturally in our hearts. Sticky love? More like stinky love. Fickle love. Heartbreak love. An enduring, never-ending love? The average person would give anything to receive that kind of love, much less fantasize they could provide it. How different is God's sticky love!

Beloved, let us love one another, for love is from God, and whoever loves has been born of God and knows God. Anyone who does not love does not know God, because God is love. In this the love of God was made manifest among us, that God sent his only Son into the world, so that we might live through him. In this is love, not that we have loved God but that he loved us and sent his Son to be the propitiation for our sins. Beloved, if God so loved us, we also ought to love one another. No one has ever seen God; if we love one another, God abides in us and his love is perfected in us. (1 John 4:7–12)

Love isn't sourced in us. Love is from God (v. 7). We naturally don't have sticky love. We get it from God. Love is merely a word to describe the energy of self-giving commitment to one another found in the triune Godhead. God the Father eternally loves God the Son and Spirit. The Son and the Spirit do the same toward the Father. This energy is like a furnace eternally burning within the Trinity. In this way, God is eternal sticky love. This divine love was revealed to us in Christ: "In this the love of God was made manifest among us, that God sent his only Son into the world" (v. 9). What did Christ do on the cross? He loved us like He has loved the Father for eternity. He gave His life for the eternal good and joy of sinners like us.

When we believe in Jesus for our salvation, God's love takes residence within us (abides in us) by the Holy Spirit. As we love others like Christ loved us, God's eternal love is perfected in us. Like a cake fully baked in the oven, God's love is perfectly matured in us. In other words, our natural loves are nonstick. They are fickle and self-oriented and don't last. But God's love is a different love entirely.

Sticky human love is sourced in the eternal, unchanging nature of God. It is enduring because God's love never ceases. It doesn't fail because God doesn't fall down. His love is enduring, and our expressions of love toward one another can be and ought to be very sticky. We love when we sacrificially give of ourselves to others.

Once again, Augustine is insightful when he says, "I mean by charity that affection of the mind which aims at the enjoyment of God for His own sake, and the enjoyment of one's self and one's neighbor in subordination to God."[5] Such is divine sticky love in and through us.

THE NECESSITY OF STICKY LOVE TOWARD OTHERS

Here is a sampler of New Testament passages on our need to love one another:

- "Let love be genuine. Abhor what is evil; hold fast to what is good. Love one another with brotherly affection. Outdo one another in showing honor." (Rom. 12:9–10)
- "Above all, keep loving one another earnestly, since love covers a multitude of sins." (1 Peter 4:8)
- "A new commandment I give to you, that you love one another: just as I have loved you, you also are to love one another. By this all people will know that you are my disciples, if you have love for one another." (John 13:34–35)
- "with all humility and gentleness, with patience, bearing with one another in love." (Eph. 4:2)
- "And above all these put on love, which binds everything together in perfect harmony." (Col. 3:14)

You likely nod your head at these verses. So do I. The great challenge for the Christian is to express this love toward real, fallible, imperfect people in our lives. Loving one another is a great principle, but we're not called to love principles; we are called to love people—people as flawed and as filled with contradictions as we are.

WE ARE CALLED TO LOVE PEOPLE— PEOPLE AS FLAWED AND AS FILLED WITH CONTRADICTIONS AS WE ARE.

HOW TO EXPRESS STICKY LOVE

Sticky love is a soul resolution to treat others the way God has treated me

In other words, the model and inspiration for this can't come from us. If it does, it won't last long because everything human-generated is temporary and self-oriented. The good news of Christianity is that God didn't love us like we love each other. He loved us with eternal Trinitarian love. God-love. We must get all the sentimental nonsense out of our minds. "Greater love has no one than this, that someone lay down his life for his friends" (John 15:13). Love is epitomized by a bloody and dying Savior gasping for air and crying out, "Forgive them, for they know not what they do" (Luke 23:34). What is love? Love is the cross. Love is willing pain. There is little sentimental about it.

The more we understand and tremble under God's grace to us in Christ, and Christ's love to us on the cross, the more that love will be perfected in us. The more that matures in me, the more it shapes how I love others. Conversely, the less I appreciate Christ, His cross, and the gospel, the less I'll care about how I treat others and the less sticky my love will be. If your love for God and others seems to wane, meditate on sin, grace, crucifixion, mercy, hell, eternal life, and heaven. The gospel makes us sticky.

Love is a fruit of the Spirit and a sign of genuine salvation

Since love is a fruit of the Spirit (Gal. 5:22–23) and evidence of genuine salvation, what explains so much non-enduring love among professing Christians? None of us love perfectly; I have plenty of love failures in my closet. But we can ask, Is the general direction of our lives increasingly sticky love toward people? This is not an optional Christian quality but evidence of genuine salvation.

> If anyone says, "I love God," and hates his brother, he is a liar; for he who does not love his brother whom he has seen cannot love God whom he has not seen. (1 John 4:20)

Godlike, sticky love is a repeated criterion for assurance of salvation in 1 John. How do you know whether you are saved or not? If you think you're saved because you prayed a prayer, had some religious experience, or believe in God or something else, your assurance is looking in the wrong place. There are biblical evidences of regeneration. One of the key ones is that our lives are marked by love, not as the basis of our salvation but as the evidence of it.

OUR LIVES ARE MARKED BY LOVE, NOT AS THE BASIS OF OUR SALVATION BUT AS THE EVIDENCE OF IT.

Non-sticky love for one another says something about God that isn't true

God is love. God's love for us never ends. Paul looks at love eschatologically, from the perspective of eternity. Love is the greatest because love is the most permanent. Why is love the most permanent? Because God is love, and the eternality of His love defines us. When Christian relationships, marriages, and friendships shatter into division, rancor, and hate, it grieves God because it tells the world something about Him that isn't true. It says love ends. Love is fleeting. Love doesn't matter. It is disposable.

However imperfectly, all Christian relationships *must* strive to love one another as God loved us. We need to stick together. This requires a growing comfort with regular confession and forgiveness to one another. We need to be comfortable with disagreeing on secondary matters. We need these essential life skills for sticky love to do its excellent work. Loneliness can only be overcome by mending the breaches that divide us from people. The degree to which we are good at this is the degree to which meaningful relationships can and will be sustained. The ache of loneliness can compel us to have the hard conversations necessary for relationships to last.

Radical love has always been the hallmark of Christianity. Aristides, a Christian apologist in first-century Athens, described Christians to the Roman Emperor Hadrian this way: "They love one another, and from widows they do not turn away their esteem; and they deliver the orphan from him who treats him harshly. And he, who has, gives to him who has not, without boasting. And when they see a stranger, they take him in to their homes and rejoice over him as a very brother."[6] Does this Roman Christian love sound sticky? Magnanimous? Godlike? It must, for we are children of God, and His nature, by the Spirit, dwells in us.

While this chapter emphasizes how relationships should be, we must live with the reality that human love is too often not this way. Rather than sticky, it's like that nonstick pan in your kitchen. How do we feel when a relationship we value is clearly disposable to the other? This is one of the hardest experiences in life. As a pastor, I am often astonished and dismayed when people I have poured into walk away. It reveals that my sense of our relationship was very different than theirs. It is extremely hard not to allow calluses to form over our hearts.

We have become relational consumers—in relationship with others as long as we derive benefit. The result is historic levels of loneliness and alienation. What should we do? As the title of the chapter urges, give the love you long for. We must invert all these loneliness longings. Take the hurt of how someone failed to love you faithfully and let it motivate you to love others in the opposite way. Follow the example and form of Christ's love for us, and there will always be opportunities to give the love we long for.

Love doesn't fail, and it doesn't fall down. It doesn't give up! It draws its strength from the love of God in Christ, displayed on the cross, in us by His Spirit, and expressed toward one another. It's very, very sticky.

Discussion Questions

1) Who is someone in your life you can look for and "specifically inconvenience yourself to help"?

2) How does Jesus' cry of forsakenness on the cross resemble the cries of your heart? How might this affect your view of Jesus' sympathy with your pain?

3) Who in your life has loved you with sticky love? How have you loved others this way? Who could you love like this?

6

Hospitality of the Heart

EARLIER IN THE BOOK, I mentioned bed-rotting and doom-scrolling. They are both contemporary forms of escapism from life and relationships. Hours can quickly disappear as posts, videos, reels, and other forgettable content take our minds off our pain and disappointments. Culture offers a dizzying array of escape options. Do they fill the space God made in our hearts for Him and others? No. You likely realize this already.

Numbing loneliness by these and other means blunt its powerful motivation toward meaningful relationships. I remember times when the relational pain was so intense that all I wanted to do was sleep; at least I didn't feel it while I was unconscious. Yet it was always waiting for me when I awoke.

Take a moment and consider: How do you cope with your loneliness? What habits of life have quietly formed that mute the pain? You may ask, *who cares what I do if it helps me?* Unhealthy habits petrify the heart from the very rhythms of life that could turn our loneliness into a guide and blessing.

C. S. Lewis lived a single life into his late fifties. His story is complex, but his insights into the human heart are profound. Here is one of his best:

> There is no safe investment. To love at all is to be vulnerable. Love anything, and your heart will certainly be wrung and possibly be broken. If you want to make sure of keeping it intact, you must give your heart to no one, not even to an animal. Wrap it carefully round with hobbies and little luxuries; avoid all entanglements; lock it up safe in the casket or coffin of your selfishness. But in that casket—safe, dark, motionless, airless—it will change. It will not be broken; it will become unbreakable, impenetrable, irredeemable. The alternative to tragedy, or at least to the risk of tragedy, is damnation. The only place outside Heaven where you can be perfectly safe from all the dangers and perturbations of love is Hell.[1]

Since no one reading this book aspires to an impenetrable heart, what is the opposite? The opposite is the hospitable heart. The extent to which the gospel's hospitality shapes our hearts is the extent to which natural and life-giving relationships of mutual self-giving can and will minimize loneliness.

So far, we have seen *what* and *why*. Now the *how*. How does the gospel give us the capacity and ability to love others in loneliness-mitigating ways? Paul describes it well:

> Do nothing from selfish ambition or conceit, but in humility count others more significant than yourselves. Let each of you look not only to his own interests, but also to the

interests of others. Have this mind among yourselves, which is yours in Christ Jesus, who, though he was in the form of God, did not count equality with God a thing to be grasped, but emptied himself, by taking the form of a servant, being born in the likeness of men. And being found in human form, he humbled himself by becoming obedient to the point of death, even death on a cross. (Phil. 2:3–8)

Do you see Paul's urging? Be humble like Jesus was humble. Follow His example as a relational paradigm for your life. So how did Jesus express His humility? He humbled Himself by putting our needs ahead of His own. Preeminently, He died for us. His invitation to us is to enter His own weakness and sacrifice. Consider that Jesus welcomes us by hanging from nails, bloodied, naked, and entirely giving Himself for us. Jesus' weakness is the welcome mat to His heart. He says, *Come to the cross, come to My heart, come to Me.*

Doesn't a gospelized posture toward others seem the opposite of how we typically seek to forge relationships? We polish ourselves and try to project the very best version of ourselves. As any glance at social media proves, we are adept at image management. We hope putting our best foot forward will incline others to put their authentic foot forward to us. Yet this tendency hinders the depth of relationship our hearts ache for.

In her excellent book *Find Your People*, Jennie Allen urges those who want to build authentic relationships to intentionally expose people to the deeply personal, indeed awkward aspects of our lives. These embarrassing areas we want to hide are the building blocks upon which meaningful relationships are built. She writes,

Once you have found your close people, break all the rules of how you spend time together: Purposefully leave your house a mess. Invite someone to your dinner party an hour early to help with prep or ask them to stay late and help you clean up. Leave your laundry out on the couch and ask them to help you fold. Ask if they'll pick your kid up on their way over. Borrow the ingredient you forgot instead of running to the store to buy it. Bother someone to run the errand with you. Stop by someone's house unannounced. Bring someone a meal without warning. Ask to borrow clothes for a special event instead of shopping for a new dress. Ask someone to help you clean out your closet. Offer to help someone paint a room. Ask to join someone else's family dinner. (That last one's truly bold.)[2]

If you read this list and think, "I could never do that!" the walls of pride and insecurity must be relinquished for what the gospel says about you.

In the words of Tim Keller, "The gospel is this: We are more sinful and flawed in ourselves than we ever dared believe, yet at the very same time we are more loved and accepted in Jesus Christ than we ever dared hope."[3] This statement provides the internal confidence we need to be authentic with others. What God says and thinks about me is vastly more important than the opinion of any human being. Almighty God eternally loves a Christian. This reality appropriated horizontally restores our Edenic ability to be vulnerable and thereby safe to risk unveiling the clumsy, embarrassing, and otherwise hidden parts of who we are.

I have observed people throughout our church ministry subtly hiding a physical irregularity. Their clothing, hair, or stance is carefully postured to obscure what they consider unsightly. I was in proximity as a seasoned and mature Christian man counseled one woman who habitually hid her deformity. He urged her to consider this a gift from God as it makes her special and unique. His words inspired her because they inverted her lifelong cover-up.

The gospel frees us to be who God made us, as our identity is firmly fixed in what He says about us. Isn't this the quality we admire in others? Who are our heroes? They are people whose struggle is known, yet their faithfulness, resilience, and vulnerability summon us to do the same with our own challenges.

The opposite is also true. We struggle not to resent people who seem to have it all together. Their lives seem perfectly polished. Is such a life possible, and am I missing out? But how do people act around polished people? Self-conscious. Awkward. Everyone's insecurities bubble out. These dynamics keep relationships superficial. They must be, lest others see behind the veil. The wizards of Oz need curtains to hide behind.

As someone who has had opportunities to see behind the veil of the lives of some materially successful and influential people, it truly is a mirage. Sin has infected all of us, and our lost Eden cannot be recovered with money, clothing, homes, Botox, trips, accomplishments, etc. Only Jesus restores Edenic wholeness where we are comfortable being "naked" with others again in that restored Garden. As Lewis states, "Eros will have naked bodies; friendship naked personalities."[4] In Christ, there is nothing to hide. Not if the one righteous Being in the universe accepts me fully.

NAKED AND UNAWARE

In her book *Celebrities for Jesus*, Katelyn Beaty describes how famous people deal with the perceptions people have of them and whom they know themselves to be.

> Many famous people cope by using what Rockwell calls "character-splitting." They craft a "celebrity entity," a presentation of the self, while the true self is hidden away, shown only to trusted friends and family. Character splitting is in some ways healthy; the famous person realizes there is a vulnerable, beloved self that should be protected from overexposure. We are all more than the sum of our achievements and the acclaim that accompanies them. We all need communities that promise to love us instead of adore us.[5]

Genesis 2 ends with a statement that is difficult for us to conceive. It says Adam and Eve were "naked and were not ashamed." As I stated earlier, Adam and Eve were without clothes, but their true nakedness was spiritual and relational. Their nakedness was the complete absence of self-regard. There was nothing to hide physically, socially, or spiritually. We contemplate this like a fairy tale dream. We have never known such complete self-forgetfulness.

Just imagine with me a little. What would it be like to have absolutely zero concern for self? Not that Adam and Eve didn't need to meet their personal physical needs. They grew hungry and thirsty and sleepy. Their nakedness was spiritual and relational in that they loved God and each other perfectly and completely. As Paul urges in 1 Corinthians 13, love is not oriented toward the self. The needs and desires of others preside over our own. This comes as we grow self-forgetful. Adam and Eve didn't need to forget themselves as they never thought in this selfish way in the first place. They were as unashamed as they were unaware.

This is the connection between love and loneliness. Loneliness spurs us to do something about it. Yet the healthy options call us to others and the inherent risk others entail. The emptying of ourselves creates the needed gap in our hearts to welcome others as they are.

LONELINESS SPURS US TO DO SOMETHING ABOUT IT. YET THE HEALTHY OPTIONS CALL US TO OTHERS AND THE INHERENT RISK OTHERS ENTAIL.

Salvation in Christ restores our ancient capacity to think less of ourselves. Our restoration to God's favor and acceptance makes less hiding and more relational vulnerability feasible. Gospel-empowered vulnerability allows others to shed their masks and veils too. How would you rate your present relational vulnerability? The depth of your relationships directly equals your willingness to uncover the real you. By doing so, you signal to the other person that it's safe for them to reciprocate. This openness of life and heart is called hospitality.

UN-LONELY GOSPEL HOSPITALITY

Romans 15:7 is a verse with profound implications for loneliness: "Therefore welcome one another as Christ has welcomed you, for the glory of God." The apostle gives remarkable guidance for solving loneliness. The paradigm of Christ's welcome to us in the gospel should be applied to our relational welcome to others.

When you are in a public space, take a look around. Like you, these people hustling and bustling near you are image bearers of

God. While this is our daily context, we can easily overlook each as unique. Each of them is a soul created for a relationship with God. The myriad of experiences in their life has never been lived except by them. There are no two humans fully alike, yet each one needs the same salvation provided by Jesus. Are any of them too high or low or different from you to exclude from the hospitality of your heart? Paul urges us to be as welcoming as Jesus is welcoming. In other words, each is a potential friend worthy of our heart's hospitality.

The gospel should keep us from any exclusion based on differences. If God welcomes them in Christ, who are we to be more exclusive than the holy God? We tend to look for someone who seems like us. We create these grids that people must pass through: similar life stages, family status, economic status, interests, or hobbies. On and on it can go. By the time we filter people through all our preferences, only a few make it. Then we conclude, "These people are unfriendly." Even this reveals our insecurities as we need every possible sameness to risk relationships. We are often too insecure to risk friendship with someone even a few degrees different than us.

Another way we cope with loneliness is to project self-sufficiency. *I don't need anyone. I've got all the friendship anyone could want!* Men are often terrible at this. Studies show that many men can't name a close friend.[6] Yet here we are dealing with our old nemesis "self." Self-sufficiency is a broken and deficient humanity. We were created for dependency on God and others. The gospel provides a path out of self-orientation but does so painfully. The gospel breaks our grip on self and requires a dependence on God's provision in Christ. This brokenness, this repentance, brokers humility. Jesus calls it being poor in spirit (Matt. 5:3) and says it is required for those who enter His blessed kingdom. The blessing is first God's blessing. Yet it continues to bless in horizontal ways as the poor in spirit are blessed with a wide array of friendships because nobody is beneath them or beyond them. Is some aspect of your loneliness self-inflicted because your self-image is too rich, exalted, or fearful, which hinders life-giving friendships? Pursue hospitality of the heart that flows from a life shaped by the gospel.

RADICAL ORDINARY HOSPITALITY

Rosaria Butterfield coined the phrase "radical ordinary hospitality" in her remarkable book *The Gospel Comes with a House Key*. Customary Christian hospitality seems radical in our culture. Rather than pulling ourselves together for a one-off hospitality moment, make it ordinary as an ongoing, daily practice.

And the gospel also comes with a heart key. We take our heart's hospitality with us. As Jesus powerfully taught in His parable of the good Samaritan, loving our neighbor goes far beyond the walls of our home or apartment. The Samaritan looked at the robbed and beaten Jew and was filled with compassion. The Greek word for compassion means to be moved down in your bowels. This was a Hebrew idiom for that feeling in the pit of our stomach. To be human is to feel "deeply." This neighborly love extends itself toward people.

LOSING OURSELVES IS THE PATH TO LOSING OUR LONELINESS. IT IS GAINING BY LOSING.

In our individualized society, this is radical. Within the sphere of gospel living, it can be normalized if our identity in Christ helps us shed our fears and orient toward others. The gospel opens our eyes and makes the self vulnerable. As we invert our natural desire to be loved and choose to love and serve others, the love of God *through* us lessens the loneliness *in* us.

Can you see how the gospel provides the means to lose our loneliness? Losing ourselves is the path to losing our loneliness. It is gaining by losing.

FIND A GOSPEL-CENTERED CHURCH

God's provision to a lonely world is a local, spiritually healthy, gospel-preaching, community-serving, one-another-loving local church. My strong encouragement is to use your horizontal loneliness to motivate strong involvement in a local church. If you need a resource to find one, I recommend starting with the church directory found on The Gospel Coalition website (thegospelcoalition.org/churches/). It is the resource I commend to members of our church who are moving out of our area. As Christians, our tribe is any genuine follower of Jesus. These gospel birds of a feather flock together in local congregations found worldwide. There is likely an organized congregation like this in proximity to you.

Look at Jesus' upper room teaching in John 13–17. It begins with Jesus washing their feet and ends with Jesus praying for their unity and love for one another:

> "I do not ask for these only, but also for those who will
> believe in me through their word, that they may all be one,
> just as you, Father, are in me, and I in you, that they also may
> be in us, so that the world may believe that you have sent me.
> The glory that you have given me I have given to them, that
> they may be one even as we are one, I in them and you in me,

that they may become perfectly one, so that the world may know that you sent me and loved them even as you loved me." (John 17:20–23)

In these verses, Jesus aims at the effect Christian relational harmony has on the unbelieving world. Our unity helps the world realize Jesus' mission and love. How so? Life in this harsh world is hardly an experience of harmonious relationships. We live in a divisive and cantankerous world. Drive on any major city interstate and you will learn everything you need to about human nature. Go too slow, and semis threaten to run you over. The billboards are filled with lawyers who encourage you to sue others, businesses that exploit women, casinos manipulating greed. On display is fallen humanity, marketing everything that shatters us relationally and spiritually. Such is the human condition ever since Adam and Eve blamed each other so long ago.

Jesus prays and envisions an alternative human experience. Instead of divisiveness, unity. Instead of bitterness, forgiveness. Instead of hate, love. A context for human relationships that restores human harmony that hasn't been seen since our forefathers ate the forbidden fruit. Where is that? The church of Jesus Christ. A community of people united in Christ, and relational harmony with each other, is a powerful testimony to a divided world regarding the power of the gospel of Jesus Christ. Sin divides. The gospel unites, even across social, racial, and political lines that historically have divided us.

Further, the experience of a healthy local church is guided by fifty-nine exhortations in the New Testament to relational fullness, often called "the one-anothers" (see this endnote for the complete list).[7] Who can look at that list and not think, *That sounds like what I'm looking for*? When a local church is on its A-game, there are no better people to do life with. It can be this for you if you assimilate into a church personally ready to provide the one-anothers rather than receive them. Remember, killing loneliness requires counterintuitive living. It is only when we give ourselves that God's love flows through us and diminishes the loneliness in us.

JESUS' HEART WAS AND IS HOSPITABLE TO SERIOUSLY FLAWED PEOPLE LIKE YOU AND ME.

Over the couple of decades I have served as a pastor, I have observed many sincere Christians sacrificing a good church experience for the sake of the dreamy perfect one. As Dietrich Bonhoeffer writes, "Those who love their dream of a Christian community more than the Christian community itself become destroyers of that Christian community even though their personal intentions may be ever so honest, earnest, and sacrificial."[8] We should be glad Jesus didn't require people of His status and spiritual maturity to be His disciples and friends. His heart was and is hospitable to seriously flawed people like you and me.

If this is a struggle, identify the pride that lurks behind the dream and engage the real and flawed people around you. And hope they don't hold your flaws against you either. Every church has imperfections hiding behind its professional websites and social media. Every single one!

Further, these imperfections are the space where communal authenticity creates true Christian community. It is not the perfections of community that unite us; it is resilient service and love in the ups and downs of church life that do. We cannot experience authentic community if we pursue it first. It must be secondary. As James Wilhoit points out, "We know the maxim 'If you pursue happiness, you'll never find it.' We discover happiness as the by-product of other pursuits. Happiness will forever elude us when we pursue it directly. Likewise, we generally find healing and support in community when they are not our primary aim."[9]

A CHRISTIAN'S NUCLEAR
OPTION ⟶ HAVING CHRIST

When all else fails, or better, before everything else fails, our nuclear weapon for loneliness is the reality that we are maximally blessed to be known and loved by Christ. Christian, you may not have a spouse, but you have Christ. You may be separated from your family, but you have Christ. You may be a widow, but you have Christ. Your spouse or friend or sibling may reject you, but you have Christ. And since you and I are made for Him, to have Him is a guarantee that someday I won't ever feel lonely again.

Our ultimate hope isn't a new relationship, friendship, or romance. Our hope must be in the full realization of who we already have. In our moments of desperate loneliness, the Lord is there, and He is a faithful guide through the valley of loneliness. In this way, loneliness is a precious gift. We should rejoice that the best of this life leaves us wanting something more and better.

As wonderful as these earthly relationships are, the fact that they don't ultimately satisfy makes God's promises to satisfy us forever even more extraordinary. Every loneliness on earth is an internal confirmation that our greatest relational joys lie ahead of us. Absence should make the heart . . . look forward.

This doesn't eliminate the pain of loneliness, but it does assure us that this pain is part of a fleeting world that is passing away. Our future is entirely free of loneliness and filled with relational fullness far beyond what we can imagine. The next time loneliness shows up, thank God that your loneliness reminds you of the glory of what lies ahead for you with Him. In this way, you can redeem loneliness as a friend and a guide for your soul to find its rest in Him.

Discussion Questions

1) Is some aspect of your loneliness self-inflicted because your self-image is too rich, exalted, or fearful, hindering life-giving friendships?

2) What is a practical way you can pursue hospitality of the heart that flows from a life shaped by the gospel?

3) Why does customary Christian hospitality seem radical in our culture? How can you make this hospitality an ongoing, daily practice rather than a one-off hospitality moment?

Loneliness and Marital Status

MY JOURNEY THROUGH LONELINESS involved a couple of decades of pondering loneliness from the perspective of a single adult. I am now in my second decade of marriage. Many people mistakenly think, "Steve hasn't been lonely since he married. How nice." Wrong. Dead wrong. This has nothing to do with the quality of my marriage and has everything to do with understanding loneliness properly.

As we have seen, loneliness is not a sin but the fruit of sin. It is latent in the human heart as a kind of relational conscience indicating what is not healthy vertically with God and horizontally with others. Marriage is the partial restoration of Edenic harmony, at least when a husband and wife love each other well. Yet it carries with it relational burdens and responsibilities that singleness doesn't. These freedoms caused the apostle Paul to urge singles to be realistic about marriage and singleness. The duties of marriage carry with them personal sacrifices and anguish, many of which do not make life easier or existentially better.

So many struggles with loneliness revolve around marriage, singleness, divorce, and perceptions of another status being less lonely. Since my story includes decades as both single and married, in this chapter, I will reflect on the pros and cons to encourage you to see both as a gift from God.

Pastors deal with these tensions constantly as we shepherd people who deal with them too. This led Pastor D. James Kennedy to summarize most pastoral counseling as single people wanting to be married and married people wanting to be single. Loneliness in marriage led psychologist and author Dan Kiley to coin the term "living-together loneliness" or LTL. The apostle Paul dealt with issues like LTL in the churches under his care. Paul does a cost-benefit analysis of singleness and marriage with these words in 1 Corinthians,

> I want you to be free from anxieties. The unmarried man is anxious about the things of the Lord, how to please the Lord. But the married man is anxious about worldly things, how to please his wife, and his interests are divided. And the unmarried or betrothed woman is anxious about the things of the Lord, how to be holy in body and spirit. But the married woman is anxious about worldly things, how to please her husband. I say this for your own benefit, not to lay any restraint upon you, but to promote good order and to secure your undivided devotion to the Lord. (1 Cor. 7:32–35)

While Paul doesn't have loneliness singularly in view, he clearly doesn't view singleness as an inferior relational status to marriage.

There is speculation about Paul himself. He was single when he wrote 1 Corinthians. Some suggest Paul, as a member of the Pharisees, would indeed have been married previously. Perhaps he was a widower, or maybe his wife did not embrace his new faith in Christ and left him because of it. We don't know. Yet Paul's insights sound like an insider, and his comparisons between marital statuses resonate with most, if not all, who have ever been married. Loneliness lingers in both statuses but in different ways. Here are Paul's and my pastoral reflections on the differences and blessings of each.

SINGLENESS

I won't pretend that my experience is the same for everyone, as no two are exactly alike. Yet, as Paul admonishes, the broad categories are a shared experience.

Time

When my interests are divided, so is my time. Ministry takes time. Relationships take time. In my single years, I had a massive amount of time to spend with people, projects, sermon preparation, prayer, and weekly emergencies and surprises. I loved the pastoral rhythms, and the amount of time I could put toward pastoral ministry would have been sinful neglect of family for a married pastor. For example, over my single years, I would spend multiple nights a week in the homes of church members. I often had people and groups in my home, as it was always available. Now that I am married, those activities have lessened by necessity.

It was easier for me to balance more relationships with quality when I had more time to give to them. As high-quality friendships are beneficial in mitigating loneliness, singles shouldn't dismiss the value of their time flexibility. Marriage requires a deep and time-intensive investment in your spouse. We only have so much time. Marriage makes sustaining other relationships more difficult. You also inherit a whole other family when you marry. Your in-laws rightly call for time investment. There are only 168 hours in a week, and one person can only manage so much.

Marriage takes time. If God blesses with children, they are a blessing yet require significant sums of time. When we get married, we trade the time necessary for multiple life-giving friendships for one primary relationship. Other friendships still matter deeply, but the opportunity for presence with them is more challenging.

Energy

Relationships take energy. Marriage takes energy. We all have a finite supply of it. In my single years, it seemed I had nearly bound-less energy. Of course, my single years were also my younger years. Still, my wife and children demand energy and effort. I slept more and better as a single. Working out was easier to fit into the sched-ule. There were fewer domestic expectations and duties.

Billy Graham acknowledged this difference in a letter to the lifelong single and evangelical leader John Stott. He said, "Thank you for your November letter. Just reading it made me a bit ex-hausted! How do you do it my friend? If you had a wife, five children, five in-laws—and 15 grandchildren, it would be rather difficult. Please forgive me if I am not able to keep up with you!"[1]

Since satisfying human relationships require sufficient energy, this advantage goes to singleness. There are many nights my wife and I are just exhausted. Other times I may have thought of invit-ing another couple to our firepit or making another call to chat. Yet marriage takes lots of talking and time. This means fewer words and less willingness to engage with others, especially when compared to singleness. No husband or wife can adequately fill our need for human relationships alone, yet the energy expense is substantial.

Focus

Paul notes in 1 Corinthians 7 that the married are necessarily "anxious about worldly things," but the unmarried are "free from anxieties." My experience in both categories would affirm this teaching. For those twenty years of single pastoring, my thoughts were substantially focused on the church. I thought about ministry matters constantly. My mind naturally moved there with problem-solving, creativity, prayer, sermon prep, etc. Those thoughts produced vision, teaching, and countless other helps that assisted my church greatly.

The married have much more to think about that lies outside of vocation or hobbies. They must think about their spouse and their needs, children if they have them, domestic cares, health issues in the family, conflict resolution, and the ebbs and flows of family life. It is simply impossible for the best-meaning married individual to match the mental focus afforded to singles. Even writing this book is an example. It takes mental acuity to think deeply about one subject. I wrote more easily in my single days. Now I have so much more to think about, and mental processing is finite.

MARRIAGE

The advantages of singleness do not diminish the advantages of marriage, or vice versa. Paul also calls marriage a gift, and it also provides real advantages.

Change

I begin with this advantage because it is the most pronounced. Marriage creates daily moments and tensions that change us. We cannot remain who we were. We will not last long in marriage if we do not grow in our desire and ability to please our spouse (1 Cor. 7:33). This is the joy of love. The highs of marriage are greater than anything I experienced in my singleness. Yet I am regularly challenged and confronted with marriage's demand to die to self. Part of this dying is the inherent risks marriage demands, which singleness does not.

When you are single, you read that teaching and think, *Yeah, I get it. No problem.* Then marriage sticks your nose in your selfishness, and, at least for me, it is not pretty. That visage brings change, spiritual growth, maturity, and a host of other helpful qualities.

Marriage does what no school or classroom can do. If the husband is worth his salt, he learns to concern himself primarily with his wife's needs and the wife for her husband. This is the essence of love and the hallmark of self-giving ministry. Marriage is a blast furnace. The man or woman enters a marriage made of one set of materials, but the heat and pressure change them. The furnace forcefully produces qualities that make not just better spouses but also better people.

When Adam and Eve were brought together in marriage, there was no need for this development of moral character. They certainly learned, just as Jesus learned despite His moral perfection. Needing to learn isn't a sin. Adam and Eve had much to learn about marriage without a single book to help them. They grew in their marriage and relationship. Such is the DNA of marriage.

Sex

Our sexualized Western culture resembles ancient Corinth, so Paul's Corinthian letter is as relevant as ever. Throughout 1 Corinthians 7, sexual desire factors into Paul's argument for marriage's purpose. Sex in marriage is a mutual right and a weapon in the fight against sexual temptation. It is at least a consideration when deciding whether to trade the gift of celibacy for the gift of marriage. Marriage's sexual freedom is an excellent aid in the struggle for purity, providing a righteous outlet for sexual desire.

Singles are caught in a quiet stereotype. You can be viewed as either not having typical sexual desires or possibly having errant ones. The assumption is that a Christian single may have some issue with sexuality because "normal" people get married to deal with it.

Really? Does God not give the grace we need, sexual desires included? Dealing with sexual desires is a matter of the heart; a marriage ceremony doesn't change that challenge. Many, many godly singles are honoring God with their bodies. Most are as sexually desirous as any healthy human being but patiently wait for the righteous context to express it. A married person is blessed to have a righteous place to go in dealing with sexual desire. Marriage doesn't guarantee purity, but it wonderfully provides for it.

That said, even this freedom can add to our loneliness if we ask of sex what it cannot provide. I have been surprised how quickly, after sexual intimacy, my wife and I can have some conflict. A single may dream of a sexual union that ensures absolute marital harmony. While it often creates exceptional relational harmony, it doesn't guarantee it. Our sinful nature doesn't take a break due to respect for sexual union. Don't count on sex to fix your loneliness. You can be lonely before, during, and after intimacy. Count on sex to fix loneliness, and it will likely amplify it. However, if you don't expect it to fix your loneliness, you will probably be pleasantly surprised by how it helps.

Emotional/Spiritual Maturity and Empathy

There is much to say here on how marriage can polish our character and deepen our faith. This does not mean that singleness doesn't have its own polishing stones either. They are different and change us in different ways. I spent a couple of decades as a conscientious single Christian man. I grew in my walk with God. I was challenged regarding my blind spots by faithful friends. All the normal spiritual disciplines did their good work on me. Loneliness as a single person is its own kind of refiner. The inner longings for daily companionship and sharing life are strongly there. These unmet desires act as pointers to Christ and His sufficiency when life isn't happening how I would like. Loneliness is a faithful friend when we see how it strips away the need for alternative or additive human identities (husband, wife, Dad, Mom, etc.).

Marriage also refines us but in different ways. The single adult may hope that the presence of a spouse and children would provide fulfillment. Married people learn quickly that no matter how wonderful their spouse or children are, they cannot provide sustained contentment. The natural challenges of sinners living under the same roof create a different kind of loneliness. Married loneliness, in some ways, is worse as the frictions and fractures of the marital union can make us long for the singles' version of loneliness. Many married people look with longing at the singles, all their relational and sexual frustration included.

I remember speaking on a biblical view of marriage and sex in my single pastor days. I received a long letter from a married man detailing how he thought I had it much better than him. He said he and his wife fight over money, but I didn't have financial squabbles. He and his wife rarely had sex; at least, I had the dream of a possible robust marital sexual life. The letter was sad and doesn't represent a healthy married life. What it does represent is how even the best marriages *sometimes* feel.

How can married people battle loneliness? The same biblical principles apply; giving is more blessed than receiving. If I am looking to my spouse to meet my needs, my insatiable idolatry of self will always feel jilted. Negative emotions regarding our spouse's inadequacies run parallel with our temptation to be lonely for a different, better spouse. Herein lies the unique sinful temptation of marital loneliness; the single person has a world of options, but the married person is limited to one. While this may seem like a low view of marriage, it is actually a high view of marriage's potential for maturing and growing us.

Remember, loneliness is like hunger or thirst. The ache and pain can be a friend if we take the energy it provides and leverage it to invest ourselves in others. There is no better place to invest lonely energy than in improving our relationship with our spouse. Too many take that pain and look to another marriage, porn, work, or children to mask the brokenness. I urge you to see loneliness as a marital gift if it pushes you toward nourishing and cherishing your marriage.

A personal example of this from my marriage (shared with my wife's permission) came when we were in a rough spot relationally. Jennifer was not receiving the encouragement she needed from me. Yep, she was right. Still, when you get honest feedback, the temptation is to sulk, deny, or defend. I had some of that welling up in me. She had long felt under-encouraged by me. But I had some clarity of thought. The sting of the rebuke was the impetus to start texting her daily notes of appreciation for her, her role in our home and family, or anything I thought might fill her tank. Did it fix everything? No. Did it improve things? Yes.

The apostle James urges us to understand the difference between trials and temptations:

> Blessed is the man who remains steadfast under trial, for when he has stood the test he will receive the crown of life, which God has promised to those who love him. Let no one say when he is tempted, "I am being tempted by God," for God cannot be tempted with evil, and he himself tempts no one. But each person is tempted when he is lured and enticed by his own desire. Then desire when it has conceived gives birth to sin, and sin when it is fully grown brings forth death. (James 1:12–15)

A trial is a spiritual challenge that can bring blessings if we remain steadfast in our faith. We are to endure trials, James says. Temptations come from our sinful nature as we are attracted to sinful choices by our sinful desires. Every trial has many potential temptations. We are not to let our trials become temptations as sin takes us down a path leading to spiritual destruction.

Loneliness is a harrowing trial. Our internal operating system is telling us something is lacking; someone isn't there entirely. Marital loneliness has many latent temptations. The key is to use loneliness's pain and energy to spur changes to our whole approach. We instinctively don't want to feel alienation. We want fullness and wholeness. Loneliness is a gracious gift to get our attention and to bring about change.

WHAT IF MY SPOUSE WON'T CHANGE?

Every marriage has a lingering sense that something is missing. Marriage can be glorious but not quite the glory we want from it. Otherwise, marriage could deliver heaven, and only Jesus can provide that. So, every human marriage has big or minor issues that keep us from experiencing perpetual marital bliss. Yet, there is a spectrum here, and most married people desire harmonious and satisfying relationships with their spouses. Some people struggle greatly to provide emotional intimacy with their spouse by choice, personality, past trauma, etc. Many books are written on cultivating emotional intimacy, and I'll not repeat them.

The next chapter contains an essential key to overcoming loneliness no matter our status with friends, spouse, church, or family: contentment.

Discussion Questions

1) If you are single, how would you describe the struggle with loneliness in your singleness? If you are married, how has marriage impacted your experience of loneliness?

2) How would you counsel someone getting married on how it changes the presence or absence of loneliness?

3) What are some practical ways you could leverage your marital status for your relational fulfillment and the flourishing of others?·

Loneliness and Contentment

LONELINESS. ALONENESS. SOLITUDE. These can be tremendous blessings in our lives. Loneliness can spur us toward God and people. Solitude is habitual aloneness for self-care and soul-care. Yet they also are easily weaponized by our sinful flesh against us. Actress Anne Hathaway, whose remarkable career includes fame, fortune, and an Oscar, said, "Loneliness is my least favorite thing about life. The thing that I'm most worried about is just being alone without anybody to care for or someone who will care for me."[1] Is Anne Hathaway afraid of loneliness? How can someone like her lack anything or anybody?

As Calvin famously said, our hearts are idol factories,[2] famous actresses included. These idols are insatiable, and our fears orbit their presence or absence in our lives. Few fears are more powerful than the fear of being alone, really alone. Why? We instinctively know that life is enjoyed more fully with others and that love requires an object, a person. Herein lies our dilemma. We need people to be happy. Yet people leave, move, forsake, betray, frustrate, disappoint, and die. It all feels so tedious and dangerous.

We all long for perpetual happiness. It is slippery, even in the best of times. Our circumstances can change so quickly. Our relationships can change in a matter of minutes. People in our lives can and will prove disappointing. Is anyone coming to your mind as you read this? When people disappoint us, the relational pain we feel is distance, coldness, and even abandonment.

On the other side of these fails is creeping aloneness and loneliness. One key factor in a sustained life of minimized loneliness is contentment. Puritan Jeremiah Burroughs called it "the rare jewel." If it's rare in your life, you are likely depressed by loneliness. The great news is that the gospel of Jesus Christ provides a source of sustained contentment even in the minefield of human relationships. Contentment is a significant antidote to loneliness if sourced in the gospel.

THE APOSTLE PAUL'S DISCOVERY

We could assume the apostles of the church didn't need to learn much of anything. They were gifted for miracles, composing Scripture and speeches recorded for us in Acts. We may see them as only teachers, not learners. Yet they were human, and only God is omniscient. One clear example of apostolic learning is Paul's testimony in Philippians 4. He writes,

> I rejoiced in the Lord greatly that now at length you have
> revived your concern for me. You were indeed concerned
> for me, but you had no opportunity. Not that I am speaking

of being in need, for I have learned in whatever situation I am to be content. I know how to be brought low, and I know how to abound. In any and every circumstance, I have learned the secret of facing plenty and hunger, abundance and need. I can do all things through him who strengthens me. (Phil. 4:10–13)

The direct context is Paul's experience of material abundance and scarcity. He has been "brought low"; this is material poverty. Paul describes times of hunger, years in jail, and the unique experience of floating in the Mediterranean after a shipwreck. He also had material abundance, the other end of the spectrum, as Christians and churches met his needs.

Paul emphasizes that his contentment was not dependent on circumstances. Of all the misunderstandings about contentment, this one is the most common. Most unhappy people think, "If only I could change my circumstances, then I would be happy." We want to upgrade our lives and think that inner peace would come if we did. Hence the hedonic treadmill of constant upgrades to cars, homes, clothes, and chronic social climbing. Even spouses can be viewed as commodities to upgrade. If not a new one, at least the hope the current one will improve to a much better version. We think, "If my life improves, if my relationships improve, then I will be happy."

THE SUREST WAY TO RUIN ANY HUMAN RELATIONSHIP IS TO BE UTTERLY DEPENDENT ON THAT PERSON FOR YOUR RELATIONAL NEEDS.

Can you discern the problem with this approach? Circumstances and upgrades to those circumstances and relationships cannot bring lasting contentment. King Solomon tried and described it as "chasing after the wind" (Eccl. 1:14 NIV). The surest way to ruin any human relationship is to be utterly dependent on that person for your relational needs. If you are not content without that friend in your life, you won't be non-lonely with them in your life. You'll likely be a dissatisfied spouse if you are a dissatisfied single. More money, more stocks, more children, or any other change of circumstance will not bring lasting contentment (not that these things are inherently wrong). The contentment of the soul is absolutely non-circumstantial.

This is good news as it means true contentment is neither out of reach nor dependent on the performance of others and is available in all circumstances. How?

The Secret to Relational Contentment

In Philippians 4, Paul calls this a "secret" he has "learned." What is it? *Christian contentment does not come by changing your circumstances to meet your desires but by changing your desires to meet your circumstances.*[3]

SOURCING OUR CONTENTMENT IN CIRCUMSTANCES PROVES TO BE VERY DISCONTENTING.

Our secular culture seeks happiness in the opposite way. They try to change their environment, control their surroundings, and manage life so that circumstances match their desires. Yet our illusion of control is constantly contested. This increases anxiety, worry, and fear. Sourcing our contentment in circumstances proves to be very discontenting.

The biblical approach is the exact opposite of this. A few verses prior, Paul urges Christians to be anxious for nothing and pray for everything. Why? God is sovereign over everything in our lives and is good in all He does. His sovereignty and goodness mean that every circumstance in my life is part and parcel of the good He is doing in my life. Since my circumstances are my circumstances by divine decree, I don't require upgrades to make me happy; instead, I "rest" in the confidence that this circumstance is a part of God's good and perfect plan for my life.

What if I want something or someone different than God's providence has placed in my life? The key is to apply my firm belief in God's goodness to my circumstances and trust God for the presence or absence of quality relationships in my life. We may hunger and thirst for more and better relationships, but can we be content with God's providential context for our lives? If so, God's peace is provided to us. We must learn this secret of changing our desires to meet our God-ordained circumstances. Otherwise, unhealthy longings and loneliness will control our lives and diminish the joy we could have in whom God has placed in our lives.

I have learned much from Jeremiah Burroughs on contentment and commend his book *The Rare Jewel of Christian Contentment* to you. He defines Christian contentment as "the inward, quiet, gracious frame of spirit, freely submitting to and taking pleasure in God's disposal in every condition."[4] From this perspective, discontentment is not only undesirable but also a moral failure. Discontentment is when a circumstance unsettles me because I believe I deserve better. And so, we pray prayers like, "Heavenly Father, there must be some mistake because things like this are not supposed to happen to me. Other people deserve this sort of thing, not me. I have done this or that for you. I am faithful to church and ministry. I pray every day. I deserve better than this."

We quickly grumble against people and complain about matters, betraying the pride in our hearts.

The gospel of Jesus reminds us that we are sinners and what we deserve is judgment and severe circumstances forever. Yet God is gracious to us and provides what we don't deserve (salvation) instead of what we do deserve (eternal condemnation). Humility is circumstances properly assessed. Further, we chronically compare ourselves to people with more favorable (it seems to us) life situations. We look up the ladder instead of down. This fuels discontentment as there are always people with ostensibly more satisfying relationships and things. Most pastors and counselors will tell you things are rarely as they may appear. Get behind the curtain, and most of what you assume is a mirage.

Christ enables us to die to ourselves and the self-absorption that strips us of our joy in Jesus. Burroughs says it well:

> Who are the [people] who are most discontented, but idle persons, persons who have nothing to occupy their minds? Every little thing disquiets and discontents them. . . . When the heart of [a person] has nothing to do, but to be busy about creature-comforts, every little thing troubles him; but when the heart is taken up with the weighty things of eternity, with the great things of eternal life, the things of here below that disquieted it before are things now of no consequence to him in comparison with the other.[5]

Often our loneliness comes when our heart and mind are focused on little ol' me. The grand story of God's love, work, and kingdom fade into the background. In the foreground is our relational hunger or pain or unmet relational expectations. A good test about whether I am justified in my level of concern is whether God values this the same way I do. If so, where does His Word indicate this as a high priority to Him? God is as concerned with our response to circumstances as the circumstances themselves. He controls the conditions of life. The question is, do we trust Him, and do we think He is good? That's the big picture.

Consider Job, whose response to the loss of all he held dear was, "The LORD gave, and the LORD has taken away; blessed be the name of the LORD" (Job 1:21). Job's perspective kept him from bitterness against God concerning his undesirable circumstances. He was content in knowing God is good no matter what.

Many years ago, a young man in my ministry, with a bright future in athletics, was tragically handicapped by a freak spinal cord injury. Everyone who knew and loved him reeled at the news. His dad, a very godly man, flew home and was met by a pastor friend. They embraced, and through the grief, he whispered in the pastor's ear, "God is good."

Is that your bottom line? Do you believe God is good, no matter what? Your contentment in the ups and downs of life will depend on a bedrock belief that God is sovereign and good in all He does. You likely feel this to be impossible. Paul's famous verse explains how: "I can do all this through [Christ] who gives me strength" (Phil. 4:13 NIV).

A prevalent philosophy of life in Paul's day was stoicism. When bad things happen, you remain unaffected because you choose emotional unattachment. *Que sera sera*; what will be will be. We retain this approach by describing someone as "stoic," meaning they are unaffected or aloof. This is a non-Christian approach, as the resources to deal with life are completely self-generated. We make ourselves content. Christianity turns that inside out. Paul is not making himself content; instead, he derived his contentment from a source beyond himself.

CHRIST PROVIDES HIS STRENGTH
FOR OUR CONTENTMENT IN HIM

A Christian seeks to live the reality each day of spiritual fellowship with the risen Christ. This fellowship is a source of strength as Christ lives with us and, by His Spirit, in us. Paul refers elsewhere to this power for flourishing in life.

> That I may know him and the power of his resurrection, and may share his sufferings. (Phil. 3:10)

> But we have this treasure in jars of clay to show that this all-surpassing power is from God and not from us. We are hard pressed on every side, but not crushed; perplexed, but not in despair; persecuted, but not abandoned; struck down, but not destroyed. (2 Cor. 4:7–9 NIV)

While he doesn't mention loneliness, he could have said "we are alone, but not lonely." God's power to us through Christ is a "surpassing power," which doesn't come from us but is from God in us. In this way, our struggles are the canvas on which God's power is displayed.

> But he said to me, "My grace is sufficient for you, for my power is made perfect in weakness." Therefore I will boast all the more gladly about my weaknesses, so that Christ's power may rest on me. That is why, for Christ's sake, I delight in weaknesses, in insults, in hardships, in persecutions,

in difficulties. For when I am weak, then I am strong.
(2 Cor. 12:9–10 NIV)

We often think power means enablement to do the miraculous
or supernatural. The greatness of God's power is revealed ultimately
when I find spiritual resources from Christ for contentment in the
trials of life. Such is the power of God completed within me. Is it
any surprise that the Christ who suffered would reveal Himself to
us in our gardens of Gethsemane and Calvary roads? God's power
was revealed in Christ through His contentment with His Father's
plan, and we find His power at work in us when we respond likewise. The strength of Christ in us allows us to do the unthinkable
and delight in our weakness. As loneliness is undoubtedly one of
humanity's lowest weaknesses, even the ache of loneliness can be
used by God as a means to display His power in and through us.
Isn't that a counterintuitive thought? Rather than asking God to
remove our loneliness, can we pray that God would cause us to rejoice in how He sustains us in it?

Like all the trials of this broken world, loneliness can be a grace
from God to mature and grow us in our faith and Christlikeness.
James urges us to count it all joy. Not that we have joy in the cause
of the pain, but we can for the result of the pain. When I think of
my decades of aloneness and my entire life's struggle with loneliness, one thing is sure: God has used it to humble and change me.
The pain has been for my profit. For this, I am thankful.

I observed a remarkable example of how God provides such
power and strength. Years ago, I visited a friend who was head-
master of a large Christian school. Unbeknownst to me, that day,
they had a special assembly. A dad was at the microphone sharing a story of heartache from his life. A local nineteen-year-old

was drag racing down a four-lane road with speeds approaching a hundred miles an hour. The dad's wife and daughter were one mile from home driving through an intersection when this drag-racing car T-boned them at high speed. The force of the impact caused an immediate explosion and fire. The young man scrambled out of his car, but the dad's wife and daughter died.

The dad happened to be driving in the area and saw the smoke. He arrived on the scene to discover that his family had been killed. Over the following months, the nineteen-year-old was charged and faced thirty years in prison. The dad pleaded for a lighter sentence. He went public with his forgiveness of the man. And the young man's sentence was lightened due to this dad's words. This assembly was the very first public event since the trial. Present were the man who lost his family and the young man who killed them. He said, "Some of you are wondering how I am able to be on stage with the man who killed my wife and daughter. Two words, Jesus Christ. I have forgiven him for what he has done." Mic drop.

Besides the students, guess who was there? All four local TV network stations with their trucks and satellite antennas. *People* magazine was there to cover the story. NBC's *Dateline* was there. All around were cameras and microphones and reporters. Why? Because this man's wife and child were killed? No. This tragically happens each week in America.

It was because this man had the capacity to forgive and love someone whom he naturally should despise. The nation sat up and paid attention. How could he do this? Where does such strength come from? Where can you derive the strength to heal the broken relationship, endure another night alone, grieve the lost spouse, and trust God in the ongoing ache of loneliness? Two words. Jesus Christ. The same power that strengthened Him in His cruciform trial will empower your heart to face any outward circumstance with inward confidence in God's sovereignty and goodness.

Day by day and with each passing moment,
Strength I find to meet my trials here;
Trusting in my Father's wise bestowment,
I've no cause for worry or for fear.
He whose heart is kind beyond all measure
Gives unto each day what he deems best–
Lovingly, its part of pain and pleasure,
Mingling toil with peace and rest.

Ev'ry day the Lord himself is near me,
With a special mercy for each hour;
All my cares he gladly bears and cheers me,
He whose name is Counselor and Pow'r.
The protection of his child and treasure
Is a charge that on himself he laid:
"As your days, your strength shall be in measure"–
This the pledge to me he made.

Help me then in ev'ry tribulation
So to trust your promises, O Lord,
That I lose not faith's sweet consolation
Offered me within your holy Word.
Help me, Lord, when, toil and trouble meeting,
E'er to take, as from a father's hand,
One by one, the days, the moments fleeting,
Till I reach the promised land.[6]

–Lyrics to the hymn "Day by Day,"
  by Karolina W. Sandell-Berg

Discussion Questions

1) "If only I could change my circumstances, then I would be happy." Why do we so easily believe this to be true?

2) "Christian contentment does not come by changing your circumstances to meet your desires but by changing your desires to meet your circumstances." Do you find this truth easy or hard to believe and live out?

3) What lessons does past discontentment in your life provide? How might this motivate you in the future?

Loneliness and
Leadership

IN THIS CHAPTER, we will look at loneliness and leadership, especially ministry leadership. I have been a pastor for over thirty years, leading in mid-sized to mega-sized contexts. These principles apply to all Christian leadership and leadership in general. All of us lead others and are led by others. We influence others even as we submit to leaders over us in various realms of life. It's easy to forget that leaders are people too. This chapter is for leaders and those who are led by them.

During the turmoil of the COVID pandemic, former megachurch pastor, author, and media influencer Darrin Patrick took his own life. With all the inflammatory news of that time, Patrick's death and how he died shocked conservative evangelicalism. He was a rising star and experienced remarkable influence as a young man and pastor. I met him once. He was very engaging and personable toward me. Despite just meeting, he gave me his personal cellphone number and offered for me to call him anytime. I was impressed. He exuded masculinity, the kind a former star quarterback (which he was) has around other men. He even wrote a book about fulfilled biblical masculinity entitled *The Dude's Guide to Manhood*. His insights on manhood (and other subjects) were so popular that the book put him in the most influential evangelical platforms and pulpits.

Yet, as Proverbs reminds us, "Even in laughter the heart may ache, and the end of joy may be grief" (Prov. 14:13). Things are not always as they appear, and our sympathies extend to Darren's family. There is a pervasive misconception for those not in vocational ministry that everyone in ministry is spiritually and relationally healthy. Recent surveys reveal a profound lack of inner health among pastors, with isolation and loneliness topping the list of causes. Lonely pastors are nothing new. Yet recent cultural pressures have amplified the problem, causing many pastors to either quit or seriously consider doing so.

CAUSES OF LONELINESS IN LEADERSHIP

While all the conventional causes of loneliness apply, those in vocational ministry (and their spouses) face additional challenges that hamper the quality of relationships that could otherwise stabilize our inner selves. I am an insider who has lived in the vocational ministry space for over thirty years. What is noteworthy is that leadership complicates relationships for multiple reasons.

Lonely at the Bottom

Most are familiar with the adage "It's lonely at the top." It is generally true that pastors are organizationally in the highest places of influence. Yet a faithful pastor is not striving for power or dominion but following Jesus' example of servanthood. The minister is organizationally distinctive as a leader and lead servant. A pastor can't shed the role, as people inside and outside will continuously see them as such. This is a great spiritual privilege but comes with responsibilities and burdens. One of them is that people often treat ministers differently. Frequently this treatment is a blessing as faithful Christians will respect and honor their leaders.

Most in vocational ministry would testify that this complicates deeper levels of relational intimacy. People want relationships with their pastors to a point. Typically the level of relational intimacy past that point is what the minister's soul needs. It is a rare friend who will go into vulnerability and relatability with confidentiality.

Very Wide, Not Very Deep

In addition to the headwinds of the leadership title, the typical leader has more people they want to connect with than relational bandwidth allows. Every Sunday, I meet around twenty-five to fifty new people, learn their names, and hear little bits of their stories. I'm curious about them, and they are about me. Some of this is my pastoral desire to connect with them and enfold them into the ministry of our church. But I am also a human being who enjoys meeting and learning about other people. What is their story? Heritage? Faith journey? Family? Spiritual longings? Interests? All of these intrigue me and compel me to connect with as many people as I possibly can. Yet I can only spin so many relational plates, and by befriending many people, I struggle to connect with even a few deeply. My ministry and personal needs mesh in a tangled web of friendships on diverse levels. The energy that going wide in relationships requires saps the energy going deep also requires. This leaves many in vocational ministry lonely in a crowd.

Stress

A 2022 study by Lifeway Research stated that of all the mental health challenges facing pastors, stress is the leading cause of discouragement and depression.[1] Without question, the COVID pandemic and intense rancor surrounding political and social controversies only heightened the stress levels for spiritual leaders. A recent Barna Group study showed that nearly half of all pastors seriously considered quitting during that calendar year.[2] Fifty-six percent reported that stress was the leading factor in their desire to quit. The second leading cause was loneliness and isolation in ministry (43 percent). Stress and loneliness partner as the inner health needed for satisfying relationships is diminished by the adverse effects of pastoral responsibilities, criticism, and the burdens of sustaining the church. The bottom line is that 50 percent of pastors will leave the ministry in five years, and 80 percent will go in ten years.[3]

Self-_____

While there are many exceptions, spiritual pride is a common plague for spiritual leaders. It manifests subtly, requiring significant self-awareness for a pastor to see it. It takes less scrutiny to see its effect. For years I had a Latin phrase prominently displayed in my office. *Incurvatus in se,* which Augustine first coined, means the human heart easily curves back to itself. As Romans 7 reminds us, the good we aspire to, we too often don't do.

Ministry pride is stealthy as our ministries depend on a perception from others of our godliness and apparent Christlikeness.

We get adept at masking our sins, including pride. Longevity in ministry requires it. Often our critics point in the wrong direction, or their tone allows us to dismiss their disapproval easily. Often their hypocrisy concerning our pride is easily observed. I know of a pastor who had a fellow leader confront him about his detection of pride in the pastor. The pastor asked this man, "Do you struggle with pride?" He quickly replied, "No. Not really." Such is the slippery nature of spiritual pride. A leader must navigate awkward situations and people while remaining open to wisdom and admonishment.

THE MORE SIGNIFICANT THE PRIDE IN THE LEADER, THE SHALLOWER THEIR RELATIONSHIPS WILL BE.

Generally, spiritual leaders are rarely confronted about our pride. This allows the sinister love of self to grow even as the pastor calls others to the humble service of Christ. A. W. Tozer points out,

> To be specific, the self-sins are self-righteousness, self-pity, self-confidence, self-sufficiency, self-admiration, self-love and a host of others like them. They dwell too deep within us and are too much a part of our natures to come to our attention till the light of God is focused upon them. The grosser manifestations of these sins—egotism, exhibitionism, self-promotion—are strangely tolerated in Christian leaders, even in circles of impeccable orthodoxy.[4]

The more significant the pride in the leader, the shallower their relationships will be. Healthy friendship requires humility, which the gospel should provide but often doesn't in those who proclaim it. This leaves God's leaders vulnerable to temptation toward counterfeit intimacies and quick fixes to the relational ache.

One further observation that I have too often observed in ministry leaders (and my own heart) is a pernicious self-pity. This shows itself in various expressions. "I could make more money in the marketplace," or "I could pastor a larger church if only . . ." or simply negativity about ministry life in general. Self-pity is as prideful as arrogant boasting; it merely hides in a "woe is me" tone to life. This is especially problematic as pastors are called to make the gospel attractive and do the work of an evangelist. John Piper adds his critique:

> Self-pity is the voice of pride in the heart of the weak. The reason self-pity does not look like pride is that it appears to be needy. But the need arises from a wounded ego and the desire of the self-pitying is not really for others to see them as helpless, but heroes. The need self-pity feels does not come from a sense of unworthiness, but from a sense of unrecognized worthiness. It is the response of unapplauded pride.[5]

PITY ARISES WHEN MINISTRY EXPECTATIONS ARE MINISTRY ENTITLEMENTS.

Leaders have a high need to be perceived as heroes—to our church, our family and friends, and ourselves. Yet, to one degree or another, we fail all of them.

Often self-pity is merely cloaked ministry disappointment. We expected our ministry footprint to be bigger, our ministry trophies to be more significant, or someone else has received the favor of God we crave. Pity arises when ministry expectations are ministry entitlements. Because the self is insatiable, entitled pastors end up embittered as no church can give them the applause their "sacrifices" or gifts deserve.

The other side is what happens internally if God provides a larger ministry context. A sense of self-importance easily rises and becomes a hindrance to authentic relationships. In his excellent book *The Emotionally Healthy Leader*, Peter Scazzero tells of a conversation with his book agent. She is connected within the Christian publishing business and knows many successful authors. He asks her, "You have been in this publishing business for a long time. You have represented some of the most popular Christian authors. What would you say is the greatest temptation I should be aware of?" "That's easy," she said. "I can sum it up in one word: entitlement. Some authors have a lot of influence after they become well-known. They change. They walk into a room, acting as if everyone owes them and the world revolves around them. It makes them miserable to work with."[6]

Ministry entitlement is a very subtle shift in the motives of a pastor's heart. When I have felt this temptation, I often consider the apostle Paul's words to the Ephesian elders in Acts:

> "You yourselves know how I lived among you the whole time from the first day that I set foot in Asia, serving the Lord with all humility and with tears and with trials that happened to me through the plots of the Jews. . . . But I do not account my life of any value nor as precious to myself, if only I may finish my course and the ministry that I received from the Lord Jesus, to testify to the gospel of the grace of God. . . . I coveted no one's silver or gold or apparel. You yourselves know that these hands ministered to my necessities and to those who were with me. In all things I have

shown you that by working hard in this way we must help the weak and remember the words of the Lord Jesus, how he himself said, 'It is more blessed to give than to receive.'" (Acts 20:18–19, 24, 33–35)

Paul modeled unentitled ministry. He reminds the elders that his ministry was not receiving but giving. He gave his sweat, time, and tears to provide for himself and give of himself for their spiritual good. Ministry entitlement turns that upside down. It turns people into means to a selfish end rather than selflessness as the means to their joy.

SELF AND THE CHAOS SELF-LOVE CREATES ARE AMONG THE MOST PREVALENT CAUSES OF PASTORAL LONELINESS.

Self and the chaos self-love creates are among the most prevalent causes of pastoral loneliness. If only we could get over ourselves and die to ourselves, as Christ taught and modeled. Only then will authentic and fulfilling relationships grow out of the soil of gospel humility.

Fear of Vulnerability

When asked to speak at the twentieth anniversary of my first church, Dr. James Grier described pastoral ministry as the terror of being discovered as the frauds we know ourselves to be. While this may seem an overstatement, it highlights one common hindrance to emotionally healthy pastors: the fear of vulnerability. While this certainly varies depending on personality, family of origin, and congregational expectations, at the core is identity. It is difficult for pastors to separate ministerial and personal identities. We wear the pastoral hat everywhere we go.

For example, I ran a few errands around our community a few

hours before composing this chapter. Dropping off a vehicle at the auto shop included a conversation with their employee about our church services yesterday. A quick stop at a department store became a long conversation with a church attendee about their family problems. All of this while on my day off from pastoral duties.

Most pastors would agree that it is challenging to untether from the role of pastor. Over time, the role becomes the identity. Unlike most other vocations, a pastor's "job" requires moral and spiritual credibility in the church and community. Yet the pastor experiences all the weaknesses, temptations, and most of the failings of his flock. Some pastors cope with this by a tell-all approach to preaching, which some in the congregation appreciate. But over time, the public airing of personal struggles can undermine the credibility and testimony of the pastor and turn gospel preaching into a group therapy session. As William Willimon humorously titled an article on this subject, "Naked Preachers Are Distracting."

While some are excessively vulnerable, most pastors skew the opposite way: excessive hiding. As the basis of all relationships is trust, leaders struggle to find relationships of trust in which healthy vulnerability feels safe. Compounding the problem is the prevalence of betrayal in most pastors' stories. It's challenging to have a Jonathan after you've had an Absalom. The longer I have been in ministry, the more Absaloms I compile. It isn't easy to trust again after you are betrayed.

WHY ALLOW ONE OR TWO ABSALOMS (WHICH WE ARE GUARANTEED TO HAVE) TO KEEP US FROM THE ENRICHMENT OF A LIFE FILLED WITH JONATHANS?

The path of least resistance is to function more and more solo lest we feel the sting of relational treachery again. One pastoral resource wisely counsels, "The greater obstacle, however, is overcoming the temptation to allow one failure to influence every other relationship. The resulting suspicion can lead us to withdraw, harming the intimacy we had previously enjoyed with other friends."[7] How many people involved in ministry never recover from relational treachery? One counselor challenged me in my struggle to overcome betrayal: "Why are you letting this person live rent free in your brain?" Indeed. The kingdom of God is vast, filled with potentially life-giving loyal friendships. Why allow one or two Absaloms (which we are guaranteed to have) to keep us from the enrichment of a life filled with Jonathans?

Gospel ministry is intensely people-oriented yet is often lonely. The causes are both external and internal to the minister. The evidence is seen in surveys showing ministerial loneliness as a prevailing hindrance to emotionally healthy pastors. The current epidemic of pastoral resignations could be substantially curtailed if pastors and congregations understood the unique relational challenges of pastoral ministry and intentionally sought to mitigate them.

GOSPEL CURES FOR LONELINESS IN LEADERSHIP

Adapting a familiar adage, loneliness in leadership is not a problem to be solved but a tension to be managed. Ecclesiastes states that life and ministry have seasons and purposes under God's sovereign eye. God has placed these relational longings in us to urge us toward the human flourishing He designed for us and redeems in us through Christ. There is no final and foolproof solution to ministerial loneliness. Like grief, it will suddenly seize us in its grip with no apparent reason or resolution. Still, it can be managed by the same means of inner flourishing everyone must assimilate to mitigate loneliness.

Pastor or leader, we are not so special. We are not the only ones who tell people to live by principles that, too often, we don't apply to our personal choices. Yet the gospel provides all the counterbalances for every cause of loneliness. Each cause has a gospel cure if pastors assimilate into their personal lives the message we apply to our people's lives.

Our modern world has a dizzying array of medical preventions for diseases and illnesses. Many of these are antidotes and antibodies that conform to the viral shape to neutralize it. What the gospel, by the Spirit, provides to Christian leaders are character qualities that can offset the causes of loneliness. If you review the above causes, at the core of each of these causes is some form of pride. Self-love expresses itself in different ways in different people. For some, it's a bombastic personality or domineering leadership style. For others, it's a tendency to wallow in self-pity or perhaps bitterness for a less-than-hoped-for scope and scale of ministry. As diseases are widely different, so are the indirect expressions of pastoral pride. Yet the gospel of Jesus Christ provides the antidote that life-giving relationships require.

THE GOSPEL OF JESUS CHRIST PROVIDES THE ANTIDOTE THAT LIFE-GIVING RELATIONSHIPS REQUIRE.

We must apply the gospel to ourselves. The gospel humbles sinners, and pastors are merely enlightened sinners. As the Puritans urged, we must preach the gospel to ourselves daily; I am a great sinner, and Christ is a great Savior. As we assimilate our need for the grace and forgiveness the gospel provides, it creates patterns of inner health that minimize the ache of loneliness and make us attractive for other spiritually healthy Christians to interrelate. When we are spiritually healthy inwardly, our outward posture is welcoming to the people our relational aches need. It frees us from hiding, isolation, and people weariness. Our hearts will practice hospitality and welcome people in.

The gospel urges horizontal relational vibrancy. "Therefore welcome one another as Christ has welcomed you, for the glory of God" (Rom. 15:7). The apostle starts with Christ's hospitality in welcoming us without reserve or restraint. In this way, we are to welcome others into our hearts. When we do, God is glorified as we are a living parable of the gospel He cherishes. It is unexpected, but many people come to a local church and find the pastor relationally detached or unengaging. While not an excuse, there are reasons for this struggle. In ministry, people will suck the life out of you. The results are far too many embittered pastors. As hard as it is, the gospel calls us out of our isolation and into genuine relationships. How?

Vulnerable Authenticity

Both *vulnerability* and *authenticity* are important. Over time, pastors learn the necessary levels of personal sharing needed to win people to our cause or church. A funny little quip here and a recent family story there, and most people will view you as genuine. But lurking deeper is who we truly are. Every pastor will have to decide whether the ache of loneliness hurts enough to open our true selves to the true selves of others. This requires courage and vulnerability. It also requires us to overcome vocational concerns that others would know the dark places in our souls.

Yet one reason loneliness hurts is by God's design. He wants us to be fully known and loved by Him and others. The prick of pain urges us into the light of vulnerability. All relationships are risky, and many people respect a sense of a pastor's privacy. This means pastors must likely take the relational initiative for friendships to blossom.

I am often open to a certain point. That point is near the level of closeness where the other person could hurt me. I wasn't born this way. It took lots of hurt for me to have an internal line of protection. It is a struggle for me. Yet risk and vulnerability are worth it when I can die to my self-preservation.

An example of this in my life was many years ago. I met a new guy at church. We were the same age with similar backgrounds and interests. I instinctively liked him, and I quickly invited him to a time of conversation at a local coffee house. The timing was providential. I was amid one of the most challenging trials of my whole ministry. Relationships were fraying. Friendships were too. I was lonely and didn't know how this trial would resolve. As I listened to this new acquaintance talk, my intuitive side was convinced that this guy could be a great friend. My normal pastoral shields were up, but my internal longing for a close friend was also very high.

As our time together concluded, I said something counterintuitive to my self-protective heart: "I'd like to begin a friendship with you if you are willing." It felt odd as it came from my mouth. But I was being vulnerable and authentic. He looked me in the eye, said he was thinking similarly, and affirmed my desire to be intentional in our friendship. I am happy to share that this relationship budded and bloomed into one of the best friendships I have had in my life. It may have happened slowly over time. Yet my vulnerability opened the door to a more profound friendship and accelerated it.

People need to see our human side. They cannot relate in friendship to the rock star in the pulpit or the uber-wise counselor. Friendship will not take root when there is a perceived faux-spiritual imbalance. It requires authenticity and vulnerability that makes our humanity and all its foibles and failures visible to others. Pastor, don't hide behind the pulpit! I have drawn inspiration from this quote: "Nobody will ever feel empathy for you, love you, or enjoy being close to you simply because you are right or because you hardly ever make mistakes."[8]

Leader, people in our orbit respect us and our role. They will likely only be as vulnerable with you as you initiate with them. As the biblical proverb urges, whoever desires a friend must show himself friendly (Prov. 18:24 KJV). This applies to leaders as well. Pray and ask God to bring life-giving friends to you. When He does, die to your self-preservation, and take the risks relational intimacy requires. Who knows how you might bless and be blessed?

Gospel Cheerfulness

A fantastic byproduct of proper gospel humility is the emergence of amusement, humor, and laughter. The words of the Joker apply to many leaders: "Why so serious?" When we have elevated self-importance, the self-forgetfulness that humor requires disappears. Then emotionally healthy joy appears as we lose our need to have others see us as important. Very few of us enjoy relationships with self-serious people. This is not to say that we treat sacred truth, the gospel, and weighty matters lightly. This was the sin of Aaron's sons Nadab and Abihu. People must sense our deep reverence for God and His kingdom work. But it is too easy for pastors to transfer reverence for God to reverence for themselves. We revere God, but we must not revere ourselves.

IT IS TOO EASY FOR PASTORS TO TRANSFER REVERENCE FOR GOD TO REVERENCE FOR THEMSELVES.

A great litmus test on our sense of self-importance is how easily and quickly we enjoy the endless ironies and absurdities of life, people, and the world around us. As Chesterton pointed out, "Alice must grow small if she is to be Alice in Wonderland."[9] Ask yourself, how do children respond to me? Children are drawn toward people who have a playfulness about them. Such playfulness requires a low view of self or peoples' opinions of pastoral decorum. For many pastors, an hour of running around the church foyer with children giggling and following could be more spiritually profitable than most other means of grace. We too easily forget that we are human.

Thomas Dubay's exceptional book on the power of beauty notes, "Wonder at reality demands the humility to sit at the foot of a dandelion. The proud are so full of themselves that there is little room to marvel at anything else."[10] When we realize the opportunity costs to pastoral pride, it should motivate us toward the humility the gospel provides. As Jesus said, "Whoever loses his life for my sake will find it" (Matt. 10:39). This is as true for the pastor as it is for his congregation. What emerges from the lost life is that we find our sense of joy, humor, and gladness in God and others. John the Baptist said it well: "He must increase, but I must decrease" (John 3:30). I think John the Baptist enjoyed life as he was small in his own eyes.

Self-Forgetfulness

Forgetting ourselves is the inward posture the gospel makes possible. When we are convinced that our identity is 100 percent in Christ and what God thinks of us through Christ, we are freed from worrying about what other people think of us. I enjoy reading biographies and have read many about Sir Winston Churchill, who led a fascinating and impactful life. Depending on whose perspective, he was either the brilliant man who saved the Western world from Nazism or the most petulant man-child ever to lead a nation. His remarkable lack of self-absorption was one aspect of his personality that astonished those around him. While staying in the White House, after bathing, he stood in the bathroom door to speak to Roosevelt. Churchill was alleged to have quipped, "You see, Mr. President, I have nothing to conceal from you."[11] Besides the notable quick humor, Churchill's vulnerability and openness won many to his side.

> **SINCE GOD KNOWS THE WORST OF US YET LOVES US STILL, WHY SHOULD WE FEAR WHAT OTHERS THINK OF US?**

Similarly, evangelist George Whitefield and pastor Charles Spurgeon caught people's attention with their countercultural earnest sincerity (what Whitefield called "blood earnestness"). This, too, the gospel supplies as redemption redeems our ancient desire to hide. Since God knows the worst of us yet loves us still, why should we fear what others think of us? Of all people, ministry leaders should have the needed theology inwardly to produce self-forgetfulness in our outward posture with people.[12]

Much of this self-awareness flows from our identity as leaders or our concern that people view us as spiritual successes. I am not immune from this. I had an embarrassing experience recently in which I was in front of a group of respected Christian leaders, many I have admired from afar and whose books I've read. We were asked to talk about ourselves. Even though I speak publicly for a living and have done so my whole life, I felt my heart beating and color rising to my face. I was in the grip of the fear of man. I don't remember what came out of my mouth, except I remember being appalled at my disjointed presentation. Can you relate?

This is yet another reason to admire Jesus. Even His critics said, "Teacher, we know that you are true and teach the way of God truthfully, and you do not care about anyone's opinion, for you are not swayed by appearances" (Matt. 22:16). Jesus' identity was in His relationship with His heavenly Father. What other humans thought of Him was of little concern.

John captures an insightful moment when Jesus' ministry success was skyrocketing: "But Jesus on his part did not entrust himself to them, because he knew all people and needed no one to bear witness about man, for he himself knew what was in man" (John 2:24–25). How do you respond in moments of ministry success? Our temptation is to dismiss our critics and highly value our fans. Jesus valued neither. He was self-forgetful.

One cause of loneliness is tragically self-inflicted. As 1 Corinthians 8:1 notes, "This 'knowledge' puffs up, but love builds up." It is a tremendous privilege for ministers to spend years studying God's Word, reading books and articles, attending conferences, and pursuing advanced degrees. The ministry is primarily Word-oriented, so ministers tend to be gatherers of knowledge and information. Those involved in teaching grow accustomed to people looking to us as sources of insight and truth. Over time, our identity can wrap around this role in the body, subtly puffing up our ego. While this is cloaked in ministerial verbiage, the underlying know-it-all spirit repels people, especially family members. Here is some wise counsel that we do well to take to heart: "For pastors in particular, the blessing of our biblical knowledge fuels an arrogance that is at best off-putting to others and at worst devastating to intimacy altogether. Many people, including leaders, do not have any friends because they are terrible friends themselves."[13] If we need inspiration, consider Jesus, who, at any moment, could have bewildered everyone with His infinite knowledge about everything. Yet He showed wise restraint and built solid relationships with people much less spiritually insightful than He.

I once was out to dinner with a nationally known pastor. I highly respect this man's ministry. He is an extraordinary networker, with most of evangelicalism's key leaders on his phone's contact list. As we were eating, we were talking about his stage of ministry. He has served his church for a couple of decades. He has published important books on a wide variety of subjects. But one thing he said stuck with me. He indicated his personal relief to be at a stage of life to not worry much about what I or others think of him. I don't think this was hubris; this was humility.

He was secure in his salvation, calling, and ordination to gospel ministry. He echoed the apostle Paul's confession, "But with me it is a very small thing that I should be judged by you or by any human court. In fact, I do not even judge myself. For I am not aware of anything against myself, but I am not thereby acquitted. It is the Lord who judges me" (1 Cor. 4:3–4). Free is the leader who is not enslaved to the opinions of others but consumed with God's view of their life, leadership, and ministry.

Gospel Friendship

While it is an easy chapter to speed-read, Romans 16 shows the interpersonal depth of the apostle Paul. We don't know how Paul would have known such a list of people when he had never been in Rome; his warm identification of people should inspire us. The list spans all levels of society. There are twenty-six names listed, two families, five house churches, Greek names, Latin names, Jewish names, Gentile names, wealthy people, enslaved people, and freed men and women; eight names are female, and some are from the highest levels of Roman society.[14] This list is at the end of the most significant and deepest theological treatise ever written. Paul, the church's preeminent theologian, shows an amazing breadth of relational aptitude. No one was too high, or too low, for him to befriend and note in his letter. It is an entire chapter of love for people. Paul was no "hide behind the pulpit" leader. If he were in our modern setting, he would have been the last one out of the building on Sundays. He loved God. He loved people. His relational investment in others must have been a tremendous blessing to them; we must see it also as an immense blessing to Paul.

> **WE MUST SEE PERSONAL GOSPEL FRIENDSHIP AND FELLOWSHIP AS A NECESSARY MEANS OF GRACE ON THE LEVEL OF BIBLE STUDY AND PRAYER.**

Friendships enrich the life experience of the leader. Ancient church father Gregory Nazianzus, the bishop of Constantinople, spoke of the value of friendship in ministry: "If anyone were to ask me, 'What is the best thing in life?' I would answer, 'Friends.'"[15] Yet the absence of friends plagues pastoral ministry. We must see personal gospel friendship and fellowship as a necessary means of grace on the level of Bible study and prayer. "Friendlessness grows like fruit from the root of pride because the person who is full of himself will not have friends. Arrogance can also manifest in the deception of self-sufficiency, yielding a 'lonerism' that is both foolish and contradictory to the Christian life."[16] Viewing our horizontal relationships as critically necessary components of health and longevity in ministry will help lower the shocking number of spiritual leaders leaving the ministry, and improve the quality and quantity of life-giving relationships for those who remain in it.

A FINAL WORD TO CHURCH PEOPLE ABOUT THEIR LEADERS

As much as leaders need to prioritize relationships to combat loneliness, those they lead need a healthy approach toward their leaders. Often the people in the church are the only "family" in geographical proximity to the pastor and his family. For example, I am a five-hour drive away from my closest family member, with others much farther away. Many pastors are in this category, and it is incumbent upon church members to see this as a genuine ministry opportunity to their pastors and families. I offer these guiding principles to assist you (and I think your pastor will thank me for doing so).

Avoid a transactional relationship with your pastor/elder/leader

While pastoral ministry is a profession, it is much different from other people professions in which the constituency is there for a provided service. When you see a doctor, lawyer, or mechanic, there is little expectation of a personal relationship. You likely only think about them when you need them. Pastors are more like military chaplains serving the same people they live with. A healthy church will understand this and encourage the pastor to "let his hair down." We cannot always be "on."

While some of this is inescapable, as we always are pastors, your relational flexibility must stretch from pastoral expectations to reasonable expectations for every human being. Don't be appalled or self-righteous when your pastor's humanity shines through. If you always posture a hierarchical relationship, your pastor won't feel the freedom to be close friends.

Here is an easy tip: never refer to your pastor as an employee. Realize the pastor's challenge is doing community and life with the same people he serves, oversees, and leads. Imagine the challenge of doing everyday life with your fellow employees, including their families, children, and life drama. Such is the pastor's reality, blessing, and challenge.

Be a safe person

As was addressed previously, no matter who your leader is, he has already suffered some levels of relational betrayal and treachery. Those scars are brought into your relationship. Likely what his soul needs more than anything is someone safe. Being safe may be your kindest ministry to your spiritual leaders. I bought my first house when I was pretty new at Bethel Church. In God's providence, there was a key church family kitty-corner to me. They realized how this might feel awkward to me and came to me and made it very clear that they were safe for me. How? I remember exactly what they said: "We don't care if you mow your yard in your underwear; we will never tell anyone."

While lines of reasonable accountability are needed, their assurance of relational safety and confidentiality helped me relax around them. What emerged from our five years of living next door is one of the most blessed relationships of my whole life. They remain safe people, their home is a safe place, and our friendship is a safe haven.

Be available without expectations

Choosing friends is a human right. We cannot be friends with all eight billion people on the planet. Most of us can only manage three to five intimate relationships. A pastor may have hundreds or thousands of acquaintances, many of whom may hope for a more personal connection. What should a pastor do when he cannot even begin to sustain all the potential friendships? In the past, I have moaned about how my relationships in the church felt like I was trying to be friends with everyone, which kept me from being good friends with anyone. A pastor friend I know is upfront with new people to his church and tells them he has as many close friends as he can handle. It seems to work for him.

However, most pastors want a certain closeness to everyone. It is simply not realistic. Give your spiritual leaders the latitude you have in your own life to choose their closest friends. Don't be pushy. Don't be offended. If you see others in more intimate relationships with pastors, be glad for them without envy. One week in your pastor's shoes would give you a very sympathetic heart for the delicacy of pastoral friendship.

The goal isn't to be close friends with every leader in your journey but to support, help, and co-labor so the gospel goes forward. Only Jesus is the perfect pastor, and even He had some He was closer to than others. So, pray for your shepherd. Look for opportunities to encourage and bless. See your spiritual leaders as fellow humans and give grace for the inevitable failures you see. And rejoice that God's plan included spiritual shepherds who "pay careful attention to [you] and to all the flock, in which the Holy Spirit has made [them] overseers" (Acts 20:28).

Discussion Questions

1) Think of a leader you know well. What do you observe about how his/her role impacts the quality of their relationships?

2) As self-forgetfulness is critical to the quality of our relationships, how would you rate this quality in your life? Are there any habits of relating to people that you could moderate to grow in this?

3) If you were in a key leadership position, how would you want people to relate to you? What leader in your life could you relate to in the same way?

Tips on Redeeming Loneliness

THE GRACIOUS OFFER of a couple in Arizona brought me to a seminary in the Phoenix Valley. For a Midwestern-born-and-bred twenty-two-year-old, the vibe of the desert city was enthralling. I enjoyed college immensely and had a great network of friends and mentors. My move to Arizona for graduate school put me in a relational space I had never been in—unknown.

After the initial rush wore off, profound loneliness swept over me. I remember thinking often that nobody here (besides my gracious hosts) cared one bit about me, my well-being, or that I was there at all. I visited a few churches and, in a few cases, offered to get involved and serve. I was declined. They didn't know me or trust me. My friend circle was nonexistent, and church community, which I had enjoyed since I was a kid, was hard to come by.

I made an internal promise never to forget the feelings of isolation, aloneness, and loneliness. I hope this book partially fulfills my commitment to seeing people on the fringes as people long-ing for intimacy with others. In this conclusion, I offer practical tips on how not to hate or waste our loneliness but to redeem it.

PRIDE IS THE ENEMY OF RELATIONAL FLOURISHING, EVERYWHERE AND ALWAYS

Before sin, Adam and Eve were perfectly humble. They knew their proper place in God's creation, garden, and heart. They expressed this worshipful posture in perpetual loving service toward one an-other. Their words, actions, attitudes, tone, self-identity, and inner thoughts honored the other as more important than they were. This constant self-giving for the joy of the other ensured their moments of solitude never once felt lonely. They never thought, "I deserve a better friend, lover, and companion." Eve was a gift to Adam, and in that sense, Adam for Eve.

Pride perverts all the good gifts of God. Rather than gratitude, we sulk in unmet relational expectations. Romans 1 explains sin's essence as a failure to honor God or give thanks to Him. Pride is so slippery that we can be engulfed in selfishness even as we blame everyone else for our painful loneliness. As we have seen, loneliness is a gift *if* we don't resent it but use it. Not always, but often our loneliness is a self-inflicted wound as our own emotional and relational inadequacies hinder the quality of relationships we crave. Rather than blame everyone else, let loneliness put a mirror in front of your life. Ask yourself, if I am lonely, what part of this is my fault? With God's help, we can polish some of our abrasive qualities to enjoy growing intimacy with others. I believe this is why God attached a painful sliver to loneliness. The prick induces change if we submit to its prickly prod.

What keeps us from letting loneliness guide us in the right direction? Pride. Self. Stubbornness. Resentment. As Proverbs insightfully notes, "Whoever isolates himself seeks his own desire; he breaks out against all sound judgment" (Prov. 18:1).

BE KILLING PRIDE, OR PRIDE WILL BE KILLING YOUR RELATIONSHIPS.

As Lou Priolo points out, "People who are not pretentious but acknowledge their shortcomings and weaknesses are much easier to build friendships with than those who arrogantly pretend to be more than they are, quickly become defensive, think too highly of themselves, talk much more than they listen, speak boastfully, and are excessively competitive. Sooner or later, friendships with proud people hit the rocks."[1] Be killing pride, or pride will be killing your relationships.

Just as Adam and Eve hid themselves, pride urges us away from others. This may be a self-protection against repeating the hurts of the past. It may be self-pity masquerading as victimhood or self-care. Like Satan, pride poses as an angel of light. Yet loneliness whispers that someone or something is missing. Rather than denying it, let it unmask the love of self that keeps you from the relational flourishing your soul desires.

Perhaps you are like me and struggle with perfectionistic tendencies that unnecessarily complicate relationships. This is pride in a different form and will make for a lonely ride. Tim Hansel speaks the truth in love, "If you are a perfectionist, you are just setting yourself up for loneliness. Looking for the 'perfect mate,' for example, leads into never finding anyone who can live up to your image. Likewise, to be perfectionists about ourselves leads to a desperate kind of loneliness, because we can never accept ourselves just as we are or believe that anyone else could accept us either."[2] The gospel reminds us that all sense of perfectionism is blindness and denial. It is cloaked pride. Pride destroys the good our humility would enjoy.

Confess pride. Share your struggle with a trusted Christian. Be specific. Let the light of confessional contrition remove the dark self-love lurking in the shadows of your heart. I have a message I have spoken to various pastor groups on the condition that it is not recorded or streamed. Why? In it, I openly share the deep hurts I have experienced as a pastor. Among the painful experiences are some people in the past who confronted me about their perception of my pride. What they said was not the hurt as much as how they went about it. At the end of the message, I give the church leaders some hope. How do we deal with our constant critics? Are these people crazy? No. I conclude the address stating that my critics are right! I am a prideful person, and most of my failures as a person and pastor are directly related to my self-regard, self-importance, and self-love. When I acknowledge this to the leaders, there tends to be a profound hush that settles on the room. Truth be told, my pride is far worse in my heart than I even admit in my message. Yet each time I have shared this message, the result among the pastors and leaders is instant rapport.

PRIDE HIDES. HUMILITY WALKS IN THE LIGHT AND ENJOYS VERTICAL AND HORIZONTAL FLOURISHING.

What happens? My being authentic creates a bubble of safety for authenticity. It has had a profound effect.

What if we all were transparent with our failures? Not in a fake way or somehow taking pride in our humility. Instead, because we recognize that the risk of vulnerability is more desirable than the constant sting of loneliness. Is there a person in your life that you could risk such vulnerability with? Go ahead. Make it awkward. The clumsy moment will either turn away someone unlikely ever to be your friend or propel your relationship forward. Pride hides. Humility walks in the light and enjoys vertical and horizontal flourishing.

SOCIAL MEDIA COMPLICATES YOUR LONELINESS

God made us embodied for a reason. Physical proximity and presence are part of God's design for human wholeness. We are the most digitally connected people ever and the loneliest. Jennie Allen tells the story of an African village where the women of the village had washed clothes together in the river for generations. Technology and home washers came to the village. The women stayed home. Researchers in the village discovered a sharp increase in loneliness among the women. The technological blessing was a quality-of-life curse.

Social media is here to stay. It offers many benefits. Yet are we happier with our disembodied relationships? So many studies say the same thing: social media is depressive, addictive, and slowly drains us click by click. This is not a book on the proper use of social media.[3] Yet putting our relational lives in order requires a healthy relationship with our smartphones and digital media. If not, Tony Reinke summarizes the danger:

Our phones amplify our addiction to distractions and thereby splinter our perception of our place in time. Our phones push us to evade the limits of embodiment and thereby cause us to treat one another harshly. Our phones feed our craving for immediate approval and promise to hedge against our fear of missing out. Our phones undermine key literary skills and, because of our lack of discipline, make it increasingly difficult for us to identify ultimate meaning. Our phones offer us a buffet of produced media and tempt us to indulge in visual vices. Our phones overtake and distort our identity and tempt us toward unhealthy isolation and loneliness.[4]

To be the kind of person who can provide loving human companionship, we need a healthy relationship with our technology.

Getting serious about our loneliness requires us to add what helps and limit what doesn't. If you decided to spend the time needed to read to this point in the book, I'm assuming you're ready to redeem your loneliness. Are you sick enough of it to make the necessary changes? Start with seeking in-person contexts for life-giving relationships. A healthy local church is a great place to start. Pray and ask God to guide you. Wouldn't God delight in such a prayer from one of His children?

WHAT IS YOUR FRIENDSHIP IQ?

No matter how much you desire life-giving relationships, you are ensuring a life of aloneness if you have known or unknown destructive patterns. Again, let the sting of loneliness spur you to make the changes needed. Ask yourself, are there any patterns in my past broken relationships that may indicate brokenness in how I relate to others? Is there anyone you trust that you could risk asking? What do you see in me that may hinder natural friendships? Ask them to be brutally honest. Brace yourself but listen. Even a 5–10 percent improvement could move current relationships into deeper intimacy.

Do you realize friendship is an art form? Childhood friendships often happen with ease. But adulting requires friendships that go to the next level. Have you noticed how often when you get together with childhood friends, the box in which that friendship existed seems awkwardly small? The conversations are old stories reflecting former levels of intimacy. Adulthood is not satisfied with superficial friendships. This makes them more complicated. Someone has said tongue-in-cheek that Jesus' true miracle was making twelve friends after age thirty. Yet friendship is an art form we can learn and grow in our capacities.

In his exceptional book *A Resilient Life*, Gordon MacDonald reflects on when he realized his adult friendships were unsatisfying:

> As I looked critically at myself, I began to realize that I was a poor friend to those whom I called friends. And truth be told, if any of them were trying to extend lingering friendship to me, I probably was unaware. I was too involved in my work; I was probably self-absorbed; and I didn't fully comprehend what the Bible taught concerning the sacredness of human connection. I believed those who said that the cost of leading meant loneliness and few friends. If I had remained like that, I don't think there would be much resilience in my life today.[5]

Renew your commitment to the priority of friendship and cultivate it with someone with whom you have sensed a kindred spirit.

There are personal qualities that we can develop that make us intriguing to others. What gifts or interests do you have already? Any expertise in some area? These will likely create curiosity in people. Your excitement to share your passions builds relational energy. Use it wisely and humbly. The fact that we have interests is part of what makes us interesting. If you were sitting at dinner or a party, what subject would animate your personality and interest others in you?

I remember that during my single days, I was set up on a date with a young woman. The pastor and his wife, who set us up, joined us. During our dessert conversation, I asked her if she had any interests or hobbies. She took some deep breaths, looked at the ceiling in bewilderment, and finally sighed and said, "I can't think of anything!" We all have moments of brain freeze like this. Yet, I encourage you to cultivate your curiosity and enjoyment of _____ and share your excitement with others. It is immensely helpful in getting relationships going and generating friendship intrigue.[6]

The other side of the coin is essential too. In a world of people who want to talk about themselves, it requires humility to let them. A sure way to be viewed as an excellent conversationalist is to ask people questions about themselves. I again note Winston Churchill. While certainly not a man lacking in self-interest, he was simultaneously not self-absorbed. To be with him was to be with someone who seemed genuinely interested in you. People loved it and wanted to be near him. It also helps to be the prime minister.

I have many conversations with people every week. I am often surprised by how they steer the whole conversation to be all about them. They seem unaware that the conversational Ping-Pong ball has remained on their side of the table. A key dimension of loving our neighbor as ourselves is curiosity about them and genuine interest in their story, interests, sorrows, joys, and trials.

Strive to be interesting when you speak and interested when others speak. If you find people fascinating, they will likely view you as an enjoyable companion. Good conversational abilities fertilize budding friendships.

LOCATE YOUR LONELINESS IN
THE GRAND STORY OF REDEMPTION

A sobering reality of God's future eternal judgment is the unending, hopeless, and grinding loneliness. All the lasting help in this book requires you to be reconciled with your Creator. Jesus died on the cross so the sin that separates you from God could be atoned and forgiven. Our vertical loneliness is the most significant as it can lead us to love and worship the one true God through His Son, Jesus Christ. I pray you will cure your loneliness and your need for righteous standing before a holy God. You are lonely for Him!

Reconciliation with God changes our experience of loneliness both now and forever. David Needham states in sobering terms:

> When God, therefore, speaks of His presence—His face—
> He is saying much more than simply He is there. It is a
> term that underlines a most wonderful truth: the reality of
> personal relationship. . . . And the destiny of all who reject
> Christ . . . is ultimately to be removed from the face of God
> . . . forever. There will be no hope of any relationship. Never,
> in all eternity, will God look their way again. That is hell.[7]

The Christian's destiny is entirely different. All sense of loneliness is cast off at the believer's death in Christ. There is no loneliness in heaven because there is no alienation from anyone or anything. It is all fullness, no absence. Our current life feels the sting of goodbyes. As the title of one chapter of Tolkien's Lord of the Rings says, in life, we have "Many Partings." But eternity is parting-free and lonely-free. The absence of any relational lack means the fullness of all relational desires, both vertically with God and horizontally with our fellow Christians. This is a tremendous encouragement regarding the value and duration of our friendships with other Christians here and now. "We have one another only through Christ, but through Christ we do have one another, wholly, and for all eternity."[8]

Someone asked me once if we would wear clothes in heaven. I want to think so. But in truth, we won't need them anymore. Why? Our perfect righteousness won't incline us to hide anything. Indeed, there will be nothing to hide. Heaven and our eternity on the new earth will be absent the slightest hint of loneliness. Will we have solitude? Yes. We will enjoy a beautiful and restored creation with renewed minds capable of elevated meditations about God, others, and ourselves. Our perfect and complete humility will enlarge our hearts toward God and others. We will love God with our whole hearts and love others as ourselves. This non-lonely perfected inner harmony will look back at our earthly days, grateful that we won't feel lonely at all, ever again.

Discussion Questions

1) Which of these tips most resonate with you? How and why?

2) On a scale of 1–10, how would you rate yourself as a friend to others? How could you improve your friendship IQ to bless you and others?

3) The arc of redemption consummates in eternal life completely absent any relational emptiness. Considering this precious promise, how does it minister to your present experience of loneliness?

Acknowledgments

IT IS A JOY FOR ME to consider how my difficult journey with loneliness may bless others through this book. The apostle Paul expressed the same in 2 Corinthians 1:4, how God's comfort in our afflictions enables us to comfort others in theirs. In many ways, this book is the fruit of so many who have shared their hearts and lives with me over the years. Your grace, love, and friendship to me are echoed in the words of this book. Thank you to all my lifetime friends!

Thank you to Moody Publishers for believing in this project. Trillia Newbell, you were eager to see this book in print, and your behind-the-scenes labors are deeply appreciated. Thanks also to Connor Sterchi for his fine editorial polishing. A special thank you to my dear church family at Bethel Church. Thank you for your care and co-labors with me all these years! Thank you also to Bethel Church's elders and leaders; serving Jesus with you is one of the great joys of my life! I also want to thank friends who read the draft and provided very helpful input: my dad, Roger DeWitt, Bob Kelleman, Phil Ryken, Lionel Young, Margaret Diddams, Sarah Zylstra, Stephen Ganschow, and my wife, Jennifer DeWitt. Special thanks to Mark Vroegop for urging me to write this book while we enjoyed the Masters golf tournament together.

I dedicate the book to some special friends, Larry and Patti Green, Kurt and Kelly Hand, Bob and Wendy Smith, and Doug and Marcia VandeGutche. While so many friends over the years have shared their lives, homes, meals, and hearts with me, these four couples mean to me what Paul expressed to the Thessalonians: "Being affectionately desirous of you, we were ready to share with you not only the gospel of God but also our own selves, because you had become very dear to us" (1 Thess. 2:8). My love and deepest appreciation to you!

Finally, a special thank you to my wife, Jennifer, and my daughters, Kiralee and Madeline. Your daily presence in my life enriches me in so many ways that minimize my loneliness and maximize my thankfulness that God brought each of you into my life. I love you. Let's not be lonely together!

Notes

INTRODUCTION

1. Sarah Eekhoff Zylstra, "Megachurch Marriage for the Bachelor Pastor: A Story of Love That Lasts," The Gospel Coalition, https://www.thegospelcoalition .org/article/bachelor-pastor-romance/.

CHAPTER 1: THE GENESIS OF LONELINESS

1. Daniel de Visé, "A Record Share of Americans Is Living Alone," *The Hill*, July 10, 2023, https://thehill.com/policy/healthcare/4085828-a-record-share-of-americans-are-living-alone/.
2. "Infographic on Eating Alone Trends: Spotlight on Hartman's Compass Eating Occasions Database," October 18, 2022, https://www.hartman-group .com/infographics/303331831/infographic-on-eating-alone-trends-spotlight-on-hartmans-compass-eating-occasions-database.
3. de Visé, "A Record Share of Americans Is Living Alone."
4. Marc Lallanilla, "How Loneliness Shrinks Your Brain: 'Underappreciated Public Health Crisis,'" *New York Post*, August 1, 2023, https://nypost.com/ 2023/08/01/loneliness-is-bad-for-brains-how-to-stop-the-shrinkage/.
5. Psalm 86:8; Exodus 20:3; 18:11.
6. https://www.ligonier.org/learn/articles/the-belgic-confession.
7. Joni Mitchell, "Big Yellow Taxi," 1970.
8. Lou Priolo, *Loneliness: Connecting with God and Others* (Phillipsburg: P&R Publishing, 2023), loc. 125 of 841, Kindle.

CHAPTER 2: ALONE, NOT LONELY

1. Paul Tillich, *The Eternal Now* (New York: Charles Scribner's Sons, 1963), 11.
2. I resonate with June Hunt's and Howard Rice's distinctions between loneliness and solitude: "Solitude is being alone by choice. It is deliberately seeking quiet, private alone time to reflect, to be in prayer, or simply to be still and

listen for God's voice. As Psalm 37:7 suggests, '*Be still before the* LORD *and wait patiently for him.*'

Loneliness, on the other hand, is the emotion that arises when you feel that you have little control over being alone. You feel isolated and abandoned, and wish your circumstances were different." June Hunt, *Loneliness: How to Be Alone but Not Lonely* (Peabody, MA: Aspire Press, 2013), loc. 170 of 976, Kindle. "It is sometimes difficult for us to distinguish the aloneness of solitude from simple loneliness. Loneliness is feeling incomplete and longing for a relationship that has been broken or denied or has never existed. Loneliness is a painful curse, and our fear of loneliness drives us to seek to escape being alone. We call friends, we plan activities, we turn on the television set, all in the anxious effort to avoid loneliness. Solitude, on the other hand, is something to be sought after." Howard L. Rice, *Reformed Spirituality: An Introduction for Believers* (Louisville: Westminster/John Knox Press, 1991), 87–88.

3. C. S. Lewis, *Mere Christianity* (New York: Collier Books, 1952), 120.

4. Mark Weaver writes regarding this illustration, "Chesterton once observed that our walk through life is much like stumbling upon a shipwreck. Strewn about in front of us, in chaos and disarray, are both worthless debris and precious treasures. Hidden somewhere in the mess is a story. Examining the pieces one by one, we can find a small amount of meaning. But when the pieces are re-assembled, reconstructing the essence of the original and revealing the whole, we begin to see the plan and the purpose that existed from the inception." "Chesterton's Shipwreck," *The Famished Patriot*, originally published April 10, 2006, https://www.thefamishedpatriot.com/?p=2262.

CHAPTER 3: GOD'S PURPOSE FOR LONELY PAIN

1. Vicky Baker, "Last Survivor: The Story of the 'World's Loneliest Man,'" BBC News, July 20, 2018, https://www.bbc.com/news/world-latin-america-44901055; Vanessa Buschschlüter, 'Man of the Hole': Last of His Tribe Dies in Brazil," BBC News, August 29, 2022, https://www.bbc.com/news/world-latin-america-62712318.

2. Christian B. Miller, *The Character Gap: How Good Are We?* (Oxford: Oxford University Press, 2018), 229.

3. Nancy DeMoss Wolgemuth, "Unfulfilled Longings . . . ," *Revive Our Hearts Blog*, https://www.reviveourhearts.com/blog/unfulfilled-longings/.

4. *Blaise Pascal*, trans. W. F. Trotter (New York: P. F. Collier & Son Company, 1910), 52.

5. Alex Kerai, "Cell Phone Usage Statistics: Mornings Are for Notifications," Reviews.org, July 21, 2023, https://www.reviews.org/mobile/cell-phone-addiction/.

6. *Pascal*, 136.
7. Augustine, *The Confessions*, trans. Henry Chadwick (Oxford: Oxford University Press, 2008), 3.

CHAPTER 4: GOSPELIZE YOUR LONELINESS

1. Jim Elliot, quoted in Elisabeth Elliot, *Through Gates of Splendor* (Wheaton, IL: Tyndale, 1981), 172.
2. C. S. Lewis, *Mere Christianity* (New York: HarperOne, 1980), 226–27.
3. Henri J. M. Nouwen, *Show Me the Way: Daily Lenten Readings* (New York: Crossroad Publishing Co., 1992), 31.

CHAPTER 5: GIVE THE LOVE YOU LONG FOR

1. Leon Morris, *1 Corinthians*, Tyndale New Commentary Series (Grand Rapids: Eerdmans Publishing Company, 1993), 176.
2. John MacArthur, *1 Corinthians*, The MacArthur New Testament Commentary (Chicago: Moody, 1984), 328.
3. Morris, *1 Corinthians*, 177.
4. Special thanks to Kimber Kauffman for this illustration many years ago.
5. Augustine, *On Christian Doctrine*, book 3; https://faculty.georgetown.edu/jod/augustine/ddc.html.
6. *The Apology of Aristides the Philosopher*, trans. D. M. Kay, section XV, https://www.earlychristianwritings.com/text/aristides-kay.html.

CHAPTER 6: HOSPITALITY OF THE HEART

1. C. S. Lewis, *The Four Loves* (New York: Harcourt Brace & Company, 1988), 121.
2. Jennie Allen, *Find Your People: Building Deep Community in a Lonely World* (Colorado Springs: Waterbrook Press, 2022), loc. 2224 of 3226. Formatted as bulleted list in original.
3. Tim Keller, *The Meaning of Marriage: Facing the Complexities of Commitment with the Wisdom of God* (New York: Dutton, 2011), 48.
4. Lewis, *The Four Loves*, 71.
5. Katelyn Beaty, *Celebrities for Jesus: How Personas, Platforms, and Profits Are Hurting the Church* (Ada, MI: Brazos Press, 2022), loc. 1821 of 3087.
6. Daniel Cox, "American Men Suffer a Friendship Recession," *National Review*, July 6, 2021, https://www.nationalreview.com/2021/07/american-men-suffer-a-friendship-recession/.
7. "Be at peace with each other." (Mark 9:50)
   "Wash one another's feet." (John 13:14)

"Love one another." (John 13:34a; John 13:34b; John 13:35; John 15:12; John 15:17)

"Be devoted to one another in brotherly love." (Romans 12:10)

"Honor one another above yourselves." (Romans 12:10)

"Live in harmony with one another." (Romans 12:16)

"Love one another." (Romans 13:8)

"Stop passing judgment on one another." (Romans 14:13)

"Accept one another, then, just as Christ accepted you." (Romans 15:7)

"Instruct one another." (Romans 15:14)

"Greet one another with a holy kiss." (Romans 16:16)

"When you come together to eat, wait for each other." (1 Cor. 11:33)

"Have equal concern for each other." (1 Corinthians 12:25)

"Greet one another with a holy kiss." (1 Corinthians 16:20 and 2 Corinthians 13:12)

"Serve one another in love." (Galatians 5:13)

"If you keep on biting and devouring each other . . . you will be destroyed by each other." (Galatians 5:15)

"Let us not become conceited, provoking and envying each other." (Galatians 5:26)

"Carry each other's burdens." (Galatians 6:2)

"Be patient, bearing with each another in love." (Ephesians 4:2)

"Be kind and compassionate to each another." (Ephesians 4:32)

"Forgiving each other." (Ephesians 4:32)

"Speak to one another with psalms, hymns and spiritual songs." (Ephesians 5:19)

"Submit to one another out of reverence for Christ." (Ephesians 5:21)

"In humility consider others better than yourselves." (Philippians 2:3)

"Do not lie to each other." (Colossians 3:9)

"Bear with each other." (Colossians 3:13)

"Forgive whatever grievances you may have against one another." (Colossians 3:13)

"Teach . . . [one another]." (Colossians 3:16)

"Admonish one another." (Colossians 3:16)

"Make your love increase and overflow for each other." (1 Thessalonians 3:12)

"Love each other." (1 Thessalonians 4:9)

"Encourage each other." (1 Thessalonians 4:18)

"Encourage each other." (1 Thessalonians 5:11)

"Build each other up." (1 Thessalonians 5:11)

"Encourage one another daily." (Hebrews 3:13)

"Spur one another on toward love and good deeds." (Hebrews 10:24)

"Encourage one another." (Hebrews 10:25)

"Do not slander each other." (James 4:11)

"Don't grumble against each other." (James 5:9)

"Confess your sins to each other." (James 5:16)

"Pray for each other." (James 5:16)

"Love one another deeply, from the heart." (1 Peter 3:8)

"Live in harmony with one another." (1 Peter 3:8)

"Love each other deeply." (1 Peter 4:8)

"Offer hospitality to one another without grumbling." (1 Peter 4:9)

"Each one should use whatever gift he has received to serve others." (1 Peter 4:10)

"Clothe yourselves with humility toward one another." (1 Peter 5:5)

"Greet one another with a kiss of love." (1 Peter 5:14)

"Love one another." (1 John 3:11; 3:23; 4:7; 4:11; 4:12; 2 John 5)

Source: Andrew Mason, "59 Times "One Another" Is Used in the New Testament," ChurchLeaders.com, March 15, 2022, https://churchleaders.com/smallgroups/176356-the-59-one-another-statements-in-the-bible.html.

8. Dietrich Bonhoeffer, *Life Together* (New York: Harper Collins, 1954), 26.

9. James C. Wilhoit, *Spiritual Formation as If the Church Mattered: Growing in Christ through Community* (Grand Rapids: Baker Academic, 2008), loc. 4725.

CHAPTER 7: LONELINESS AND MARITAL STATUS

1. Timothy Dudley-Smith, *John Stott: A Global Ministry: A Biography—The Later Years* (Downers Grove, IL: IVP, 2001), 260.

CHAPTER 8: LONELINESS AND CONTENTMENT

1. Anne Hathaway, interview by Angelina Jolie, *Interview Magazine*, July 27, 2010, https://www.interviewmagazine.com/film/anne-hathaway.

2. See John Calvin, *Institutes of the Christian Religion*, 1.11.8.

3. I have taught, read, and listened to many sources on this subject. This represents many sources now forgotten.

4. Jeremiah Burroughs, *Rare Jewel of Christian Contentment* (Zeeland, MI: Reformed Church Publications, 2017), 16.

5. Burroughs, *Rare Jewel*, 100–101.

6. "Day by Day," trans. A. L. Skoog, Hymnary.org, https://hymnary.org/text/day_by_day_and_with_each_passing_moment.

CHAPTER 9: LONELINESS AND LEADERSHIP

1. Lifeway Research, "The Greatest Needs of Pastors: A Survey of American Prostestant Pastors," https://research.lifeway.com/wp-content/uploads/

2022/01/The-Greatest-Needs-of-Pastors-Phase-2-Quantitative-Report-Release-1.pdf.

2. Barna Group, "Pastors Share Top Reasons They've Considered Quitting Ministry in the Past Year," April 27, 2022, https://www.barna.com/research/pastors-quitting-ministry/.

3. Michael Haykin, Brian Croft, and James Carroll, *Pastoral Friendship: The Forgotten Piece to a Persevering Ministry* (Ross-shire, Scotland: Christian Focus Publications LTD, 2022), 18.

4. A. W. Tozer, *The Pursuit of God* (Camp Hill, PA: Christian Publications, 1982), 45.

5. John Piper, *Faith in Future Grace* (Sisters, OR: Multnomah Books, 1995), 94–95.

6. Peter Scazzero, *The Emotionally Healthy Leader: How Transforming Your Inner Life Will Deeply Transform Your Church, Team, and the World* (Grand Rapids: Zondervan, 2015), loc. 4519 of 5570.

7. Haykin, Croft, and Carroll, *Pastoral Friendship*, 133.

8. Allan Mallinger and Jeannette DeWyze, *Too Perfect: When Being in Control Gets Out of Control* (New York: Ballantine Books, 2011), loc. 844 of 3071.

9. G. K. Chesterton, *Orthodoxy* (Wheaton, IL: Harold Shaw Publishers, 1994), 99.

10. Thomas Dubay, *The Evidential Power of Beauty: Science and Theology Meet* (San Fransisco: Ignatius Press, 1999), 77.

11. Robert Schmuhl, "Mr. Churchill in the White House," The White House Historical Association, https://www.whitehousehistory.org/mr-churchill-in-the-white-house-1. Churchill denied making this quip.

12. Thomas Merton says, "When humility delivers a man from attachment to his own works and his own reputation, he discovers that true joy is only possible when we have completely forgotten ourselves. And it is only when we pay no more attention to our own life and our own reputation and our own excellence that we are at last completely free to serve God for His sake alone." Tim Hansel, *Through the Wilderness of Loneliness* (Elgin, IL: David C. Cook, 1991), 123.

13. Haykin, Croft, and Carroll, *Pastoral Friendship*, 129–30.

14. Thomas R. Schreiner, *Baker Exegetical Commentary on the New Testament, Romans* (Grand Rapids: Baker Academic, 1988), 727, 729.

15. Haykin, Croft, and Carroll, *Pastoral Friendship*, 46.

16. Haykin, Croft, and Carroll, *Pastoral Friendship*, 119.

CHAPTER 10: TIPS ON REDEEMING LONELINESS

1. Lou Priolo, *Loneliness: Connecting with God and Others* (Phillipsburg, NJ: P&R Publishing, 2023), loc. 516 of 841, Kindle.
2. Tim Hansel, *Through the Wilderness of Loneliness* (Elgin, IL: David C. Cook, 1991), 125.
3. Excellent resources include Tony Reinke's *12 Ways Your Smartphone Is Changing You* and Chris Martin's *The Wolf in Their Pockets*.
4. Tony Reinke, *12 Ways Your Smartphone Is Changing You* (Wheaton, IL: Crossway, 2017), 189.
5. Gordon MacDonald, *A Resilient Life* (Nashville: Thomas Nelson, 2004), 205.
6. Charles Durham lists six steps to friendship. 1. Examine and develop your interests. 2. Enter the proper matrix, a place or group where there are others of similar mind. 3. Contribute to the life and thought of those in the group. 4. Develop traits that draw people—subdue traits that repel them. 5. Reach out to others. 6. Continue to function as a group member even when you feel the process is taking too long. Charles Durham, *When You're Feeling Lonely: Finding a Way Out* (Downers Grove, IL: InterVarsity Press, 1984), 156.
7. David Needham, *Close to His Majesty* (Sisters, OR: Multnomah Books, 1987), 56–57.
8. Deitrich Bonhoeffer, *Life Together* (New York: Harper Collins, 1954), 26.

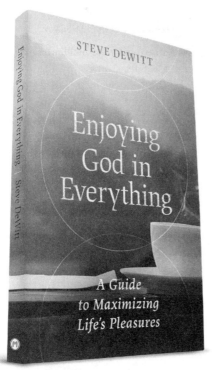

Perhaps now more than ever our lives are in need of beauty!

We were made *by* God but also *for* Him and His beauty. Pastor Steve DeWitt invites us to taste and see how God is the beauty behind all beauty. DeWitt opens our eyes to beauty's appointed end: worship! Nothing is more desirable than the beautiful One who saves: Jesus Christ.

"DeWitt focuses on beauty and how we can enjoy God in everything. Yes, everything. He wants Christians to enjoy beauty and joy and wonder and to allow each of these things to lead us to the source of all that is good, true, and beautiful. I am glad to commend it to you."

—TIM CHALLIES
Pastor, speaker, and author at Challies.com

"Steve DeWitt's book *Enjoying God in Everything* is an invitation to explore the beauty of God expressed through creation and Christ in a way that leads us to greater wonder and worship. Like a refreshing drink on a hot day, this book reminds us to sit and savor all the loveliness of God as we gaze upon His goodness."

—MELISSA KRUGER
Author and director of Women's Initiatives for The Gospel Coalition

MOODY
Publishers®

From the Word to Life®